How to Find and Develop Effective Illustrations

How to Find and Develop Effective Illustrations

The "How" and "Why" of Sermon Illustration

by
Louis Paul Lehman

KREGEL PUBLICATIONS
Grand Rapids, Michigan 49501

Library of Congress Cataloging-in-Publication Data

Lehman, Louis Paul.
  How to Find and Develop Effective Illustrations.

  Originally published under title: Put a Door On It!
  1. Homiletical illustrations. 2. Preaching.
3. Oratory. I. Title.
[BV4226.L43 1985]   251'.08   85-18107
ISBN 0-8254-3133-6

Printed in the United States of America

CONTENTS

PREFACE

The song service four-foured to its last note on the strong support of organ and piano. It broke off to silence with one authoritarian wave of the director's hand. Bert Jones was introduced as the feature attraction. Bert was a chalk artist. His three-legged stand held up a great blank for the audience's inspection. The expanse of white paper was intriguing, but meaningless. Open space without a fence. Not even a border surrounded it. Its dimensions marched off into the whole background.

But everyone knew this was temporary.

Actually they were all there to see what would happen to that blank paper. Small children wriggled up to their knees. Adults dodged from side to side to escape the impediments of hats, heads on extra tall bodies, and other children with short bodies standing upright on the seat. The lights all ran out and left darkness behind them. Then the wires put their watts together and punctuated the auditorium with an exclamation point that shouted from the white paper, "Look at me!"

Everyone looked.

Bert turned his back to the audience and his face to the board on the easel. His hands were swift and sure. He made great strokes of color across the empty page. The lines began to make sense. He was not spelling with the alphabet, but with the legible language of art. Anyone could read the picture. He was drawing a house.

The musical background reinforced the judgment. "Bless this house. . . ." It just had to be a house. Lawn. Trees. A driveway. Windows with shutters. Green shutters. A slanted roof to drool icicles in winter. A chimney breathing smoke upward and outward into the blue sky.

You could hear the little nudges running along the rows: "It's a house." Obviously, a house. The artist faded and shaded the lights, changing the colors but not the pattern. The final touch was being prepared. It was then, from the middle of the congregation, came the demanding voice of a small child: "Put a door on it!"

The words stretched out like a clothesline frozen stiff so that it didn't need poles. The laughter started. The artist was jolted for a moment, but he recovered quickly. He had deliberately drawn the house without a door, anticipating that at the right moment he would step forward and ask the audience what was missing. But one tiny girl—mine—beat him to the drawing. That's why I remember it so vividly. I had been leading the singing, my wife was at the piano, and Karen, our older daughter (one and only at that time), was seated on her Grandma Davis' lap somewhere in the middle of the church. And Karen was afraid the artist would miss the idea. She hollered out her suggestion.

Bert did as suggested, smiling with the crowd, and then made the application that Christ is the door to God, the home of the soul. Every gospel proclamation should include the gospel invitation, the possibility of coming to God. There must be a door so that men may enter. Windows are fine, but men need more than a look at God or the knowledge that He looks at them. They need a way to get together, those two, a man and God. Jesus instituted His own necessity when He insisted, "I am the door"; "No man cometh unto the Father but by me."

The secondary application, however, becomes the prime mover of this book. Every house must have a door or the outsider cannot become an insider. Every one who ministers the Word of God needs a door somewhere in his message so that the spectator may become a participant. The premise of this concept will be that an illustration serves as a perfect door for such a circumstance.

"A sermon without illustrations is like a house without windows." This ancient saw stared at me from the pages of old books about preaching. The statement can stand a little remodeling: "A message without an illustration is like a house without a door."

Windows allow one inside the house to receive light or to gaze with pity or scorn on those who are outside. Windows may furnish an outsider with guidance by light through the window. Windows may allow an outsider to look with longing upon the sight of comfortable furnishings, a warm hearth, and the joys of home; and he may be turned away from even the sight of it by drapes embracing the window. Windows furnish no means, however, whereby the insider can get out and go to work or become a minister to those whom he surveys. Windows do not allow outsiders to become insiders and participate in what they see to enjoy. A message from God is not intended to be merely illuminating, but to be obeyed. "Be ye doers of the word and not hearers only" indicates that the Word provides a means of "going in and out" which Jesus mentioned in John 10:9. Christ Himself is the door of the sheepfold of God. There is no equivocation about this. But the message which is true to His Word provides a means of obedience, of getting into the message. The minister of the truth evokes an atmosphere, an environment, a challenge— a house, if you please—in which saints see their obligations and sinners behold their opportunities. To "get in and out" of this message requires a door.

It is easy to show that illustrations are a Bible method, for Jesus used parables and Paul employed countless figures. But a Bible method of what? Not of just introducing more light but of providing an opportunity to become part of the truth. To enforce such a premise this illustrative concept is submitted to you.

ACKNOWLEDGMENTS

Acknowledgment is due Kregel Publications for use of short quotes from Weymouth *New Testament in Modern Speech* (1978), the Zondervan Corporation for use of short quotes from *The Berkeley Version* (1945) and Oxford University Press for a quote from Samuel Eliot Morison *The Oxford History of the American People* (1965).

INTRODUCTION

This is a handbook for a particular person. Many of the ideas may be useful for any public speaker, but the peculiar aim is to furnish know-how for a public speaker whose purpose and responsibility are spiritual. This includes ministers, teachers, and someone unable to apologize his way out of the grasp of a youth leader who insists that he speak to the boys' club, girls' club, or Ladies' Aid Society. The philosophy of this tract, therefore, will be Christian and scripturally oriented. To make a convenient abbreviation for preachers, teachers, and all such, we will designate the personnel involved as a p/t.

Three basic elements make the p/t's service more than a time-filler:

1. Attention
2. Authority
3. Action

Action is always the finale, for if the p/t excites action too quickly his audience will go forth to practice before he gets through preaching. There are some occasions when this might be a good idea, but it would be devastating in the average circumstance. Attention and authority may be reversed in sequence, however, without detriment. An understanding of these essentials should be in the p/t's tool box or he will be as limited as a child whose driving skills include nothing more than knowing how to turn the ignition key.

There are some basic concepts that should be underscored from the start. First, there is no substitute for spiritual power. Presenting the claims of Jesus Christ is fundamentally a spiritual endeavor. The champion of truth is banging away at carnal minds which are "enmity against God," and even in the spiritual listener we contend with the natural reluctance of flesh, which runs the gamut from mild unwillingness to violent inflexibility. We are also contending with the power of Satan, an antagonist whom advertisers for earthly gewgaws never have to bother about. The truth itself, which we spell out by the letter, needs the divine Catalyst to make it perform in the minds of men. No amount of information, no polished skills, no richness of experience can redeem from the poverty of spiritual scantiness.

Second, the spiritual necessity does not negate the value of adequate preparation and disciplined skill. In music, art, and janitorial services, the church asks for experienced, trained people who are consistently working at improving their competence. No church would hire an architect who had never designed so much as a chicken coop on the thin ice that he is a fine Christian and will be inspired to design a good church building. No church would employ as chief cook at a banquet for two hundred people a sincere woman whose only experience and training for the job was feeding herself, husband, and pet dog.

It is thought unspiritual, however, that a p/t should write, polish, rehearse, and artistically master his presentation of the Word of God. A minister preaching in front of a mirror sounds like an affront to the Holy Spirit. It is a foregone conclusion in many Christian minds that a person who depends on a written script is not depending on the Lord. The same people may be heartily blessed, however, by a singer who uses a song in which every printed word and note has been carefully rehearsed. The singer is forgiven for holding words and music in his hand for a three-minute rendition, but a p/t with notes in his hands for a thirty-minute message is deemed too dependent on human devices.

Of course there is hazard in elaborate preparation. The well-constructed, well-polished, well-delivered message may draw attention to the speaker and breed admiration for him rather than love for and obedience to the Lord. But the peril is not as great as some think, and I have met some mediocre workmen who would have been distinguished performers if they had been as scrupulous in preparation as they were in sweeping up the crumbs of praise thrown to them like scraps to a sad-eyed pup.

Walk into a room illuminated by a naked bulb, dangling like a skeleton of white fire in a fistful of glass, and probably you won't pay much attention to the fixture. There is really nothing to notice. Walk into a room amiably illuminated by a fountain of light pouring graciously from a handsome chandelier, and you would probably be tempted to remark about the pleasing effect of the candelabrum.

"Oh, yes," you say, "and there is the whole point. You lose recognition of the light in the beauty of the fixture, and that is unspiritual. That detracts from the One who should be praised."

But is that true?

Stay in the room with the bare light bulb for an hour, and sheer irritation will draw your attention to the bulb. You will wonder why it wasn't shaded in some manner. You will resent it as a crude feature in such a convenient age. Forgetting to be grateful for the light, you will grumble about the drop-cord and the glaring incandescence. The simplicity which sounds commendable becomes aggravating.

Stay in the room with the well-designed fixture for an hour, and you will forget about the elegance of that appointment. Who stares at a chandelier for more than a passing notice? It will get its fair share of acknowledgment and then be forgotten, unless it falls from its place or ceases to function. It is simply accepted.

In the contemporary scene of sophistication, intelligence, and expertise, a bumbling, ill-organized, desultory presentation of truth is not a good bet to provoke reactions that the p/t was unpretentious and Christ-glorifying. It is more auspicious to insinuate that the messenger was crude, even conceited, to imagine he was worthy of a hearing, and that he must have considered that his presentation was not deserving of adequate preparation.

"While all Christians should 'preach the gospel,' and many an unordained preacher like the great lay-preacher who suffered for his boldness twelve years in Bedford jail, may be a hundred fold more effective than one who is regularly appointed, yet even the lay-preacher should be fitted for the work both by human and divine preparation; he should not be a 'novice,' he should be 'apt to teach'."[1]

Third, perusal of these few chapters, and other "how to" books, is not sufficient preparation for anything. The work must be done by the individual. It cannot be done by

---

[1]James M. Hoppin, *Homiletics* (New York: Funk and Wagnalls, 1883), p. xxvi.

proxy or osmosis. Reading precise directions about steaming off old wallpaper doesn't clean the walls. I know. I read those plain, understandable, direct lines again and again. I was hoping the old wallpaper would prefer to peel itself off rather than making me actually turn loose the steam. But there was only a dream in that scheme; it required vapor on the paper, aided by a scraper and patching plaster, to accomplish the job.

No one furnishes ten easy lessons to replace a Bible institute curriculum, seminary training, or classroom experience. There is no one-toll highway to a better ministry. This book is a map, slightly detailed, of one area of the thrilling adventure of proclaiming Christ. It is designed to excite the p/t who has not found for himself the vast realm of illustration; who possesses, but has not employed, the ability to see, isolate, and use the illustrative material all about us.

Fourth, this treatise is for the p/t who is seriously interested in mechanically improving his presentation of spiritual truth. Obviously, no author can communicate spiritual power to the reader. The old "pro" will find these chapters shamelessly elementary. Every responsible Christian with a fleabite of leadership finds himself catapulted into a speaking engagement. Intelligent people usually can come up with one good speech, even two or three. For many occasional speakers, that's the end of it. A fellow has a winner, and he can repeat it a hundred times, polishing it a little extra with each performance. He may even do (as it was reported to me) what Will Hogg, who was one of the greatest, did with a story. At the first telling about his anger at a mule, he ranted, raved, and threatened the mule. By the fiftieth telling he bit the mule.

But many nonprofessional, accidental speakers find the endeavor challenging. They want to speak again. The tenth or the hundredth time, the pressure becomes almost intolerable. It is necessary for a man to keep his own soul fresh and thrilled with the opportunity. Scratching for outlines, borrowing from your pastor, stealing from books, magazines, and tracts—all this takes some of the luster out of the adventure. To such a scratcher - borrower - thief this book may be important. I have tried to simply and clearly delineate the struggle, purpose, and methods that one p/t has found to be inevitable, stimulating, and useful in what is getting uncomfortably close to a half-century of ministry. No claim is made for authority, unique ability, or skill beyond the experience privileged to me by the guidance and help of God. Most of what is reported on these pages is the product of a providential acquaintance with some of the most capable people that Christian service has ever possessed. A good deal of what is reported, however, is the product of a method God has been pleased to allow most of us to stumble through: "learn by experience" (Weymouth translation of Rom. 12:2).

However trite, perhaps even trivial, may appear the suggestions that follow, the aim is to improve the facilities of those who are seriously concerned about a good presentation of material which they feel is worthy of being heard. My uncle, Dr. A. E. Lehman, was a Presbyterian minister; and after his death I was given the opportunity to select some fine volumes out of his library. Among others, I took a large book of nine hundred pages, which appeared from the title to be exactly what a young preacher would need: *A Homiletic Encyclopaedia of Illustrations in Theology and Morals,*[2] selected and arranged by R. A. Bertram. I was then illustration hunting, but I was stalking game chained to other men's trees. I mistook many a tame household cat for a lion. Uncle Arthur, something of a precisionist, had entered in the front of this

[2]R. A. Bertram. *A Homiletic Encyclopaedia of Illustration,* (London: R. D. Dickinson, 1879).

heavy tome the purchase date of January 1, '11, and the purchase price of $1.00. The heavy tome turned out to be an elaborate tomb in which were interred the whitened bones of old relics, some of them sealed in ancient caskets of great beauty but no value. To drag out most of those skeletons you had to cut down the cobwebs, endure the choking of dust and mustiness, and the moment you got the treasure into sunlight it dissolved in a cloud of irrelevance. The collection had been printed in 1879.

I stowed it away on a high shelf, hidden behind Ruskin and Emerson. My plans for using that sober gray giant as a valley of green illustrations were eliminated after fifty attempts to find one appropriate item in those pages. In repeated cullings of my own library I tossed that book into the reject pile a half-dozen times. But somehow it always got back into the keep-and-search-again basket. Perhaps its venerable age suggested to my conniving mind that if I kept it long enough it might turn into an antique that could be peddled for a pretty dollar. Finally I started reading it where every book should be started, right at the beginning. I respected a man who would spend the time and effort to accumulate so much material, even if it left me cold. Therefore, I read the introduction. Point 3 warmed my bones:

"This work is intended rather for study than for hasty reference. It is not for the man who, when he finds his ideas running dry, and does not see how he is to finish a sermon effectively, runs to some Dictionary to find something that can be tacked on to what he has written; but for the faithful preacher . . . who gives diligence beforehand to find out 'acceptable words' and useful ideas. It is not intended for the idler, who preaches under compulsion, but for the earnest student, to whom preaching is a delight."

Although light and (I trust) interesting in style, with a determined attempt for lucidity, this present tiny volume is geared to the same person as Mr. Bertram's ponderous production.

There is a deadly jeopardy in the attainment of the highest. The wise man, as Solomon calls him, and what contemporary culture classes as the intelligent, the scientific, the intellectual, may become isolated from ordinary mortals. Thus the opinionate becomes lonely, and the others are left unenriched. This is exaggeratedly true in theology, doctrine, and scriptural truth. There must be a conscious effort on the part of the man who knows something to have others enter into—not just see, but enter—what he knows.

"In addition to being wise, the Preacher taught the people knowledge, weighing and searching out; he made many proverbs. The Preacher searched to find words of delight, and to write correctly the reliable words of truth" (Eccles. 12:9, 10 Berkeley Version).

YOU'VE GOT TO START SOMEWHERE

CHAPTER ONE

YOU'VE GOT TO START SOMEWHERE

In the introduction we left an outline dangling like a long thread trailing out behind a needle stuck in a pin cushion. It needs to be stitched into something so that it completes a pattern and service.

1. Attention
2. Authority
3. Action

This is the ordinary course of events. There are times when authority may precede attention or actually establish the attention because of some extraordinary circumstance or person.

Authority is found in three dimensions:

a. The man
b. The message
c. The moment

Some men have a peculiar gift of authority. Although it may not have been true at the beginning of their ministry, it was surely true by the time of their great effectiveness, that men like D. L. Moody, Billy Sunday, Henry Ward Beecher, and Charles Finney had assumed such an image in the public consciousness that their very presence was authoritative. This is seen today in men like Billy Graham, Charles Fuller, Harold Ockenga, and many others, who, at least in their own camp, are recognized authorities. Men who have excelled in the realm of business, sports, science, the arts, politics, or have received a great deal of publicity, carry a built-in authority factor. There are a few men of such commanding presence and personality that they breathe authority on a gathering of people. Undoubtedly this is an advantage. It also renders vulnerable, for the advantaged individual must live up to "his billing" or he will encounter disappointment. It is easier to charm an audience when they aren't expecting too much.

There are moments which produce authority. In an extreme emergency, crisis, or disaster, a man who can take hold of the situation may gain authority right on the spot. There is also the "on the spot" authority of a man fulfilling his own role as is expected of him. This is sometimes seen in a pastor, who, by the ordination of God and the call of the local congregation, is recognized as the leader of the church. This saves time. It gives the minister in his church or the teacher in his class a lever of influence over even those who disagree with him personally, politically, or theologically. It also explains why some pastors are effective in their own pulpits, but never rise to greatness in other settings.

The p/t who sues for what Thomas Chalmers fetchingly dubs "the crown rights of King Immanuel," is authorized by his message, the Word of God. The apostle Paul excited enthusiasm by his presence. He was implicated with the cadre that "turned the world upside down." Yet he was faithful to the prodding of the Spirit to renounce any premise of human authority. "And I, brethren, when I came to you, came not with the excellency of speech or of wisdom . . . that your faith should not stand in the wisdom of men, but in the power of God" (I Cor. 2:1, 5).

An interesting analysis might be made of Paul's recitation of his credentials in Philippians 3: "We are the circumcision who worship God in the spirit. . . . If any other man thinketh that he hath reasons for which he might trust in the flesh, I more. . . . Hebrew of the Hebrews . . . a Pharisee . . . blameless." He immediately follows these particulars with a denial of their worth: "have no confidence in the flesh. . . . Those I counted loss." A valid argument might be entered that Paul acted like a lawyer who introduces questions and obtains responses in the presence of the jury, knowing full well that the opposing attorney will enter objection and the judge will sustain the objection. The offender is aware that the advice to strike it from the record and disregard the statement is theoretical, for the episode gives sharper emphasis to the inadmissible content.

Two unavoidable facts are clearly seen by the careful reader of Scripture: (1) God does use for His purposes the authority which has accumulated in a man; and (2) the man of God realizes that his only true authority is the Word of God. That these appear to be in direct opposition to each other is another of the lovely mysteries of the ways of God, who amplifies the contradictions of the finite into the harmony of the Infinite.

Mechanical provisions cannot guarantee success in an endeavor which must calculate spiritual dimensions. The performing arts run the peril of the human performer who can give a poor performance because of illness, mental or emotional disturbance, or lack of enthusiasm. There is always the peril of an unresponsive audience. The spiritual contest takes on increased jeopardy: the devices of the enemy, the resistance of the carnal mind to the things of God, and the quality of the fabric with which we have to deal—for spiritual truth must be spiritually discerned. A recognition of the authority of the Word is necessary, but even this does not guarantee the results we desire to see. By our measuring apparatus a great deal of Bible preaching/teaching is sterile. Jesus illustrated this by the parable of the seed which was faithfully scattered, but some the birds got, the wayside gobbled, the thorns choked, and the sun destroyed. The grace of God entered savingly, however, and demanded that some fall on good ground.

Forcing an interpretation of Isaiah 55:11—"my word . . . shall not return unto me, but it shall accomplish that which I please"—to include each and every publication, proclamation, and presentation of Bible truth as distinguished from the total revelation of God's Word as an entity in the world, does not vary this fact in the least. Paul contemplates the paradox that we are to some "a savor of death unto death," while to others "a savor of life unto life," even though we do not corrupt the Word of God, "but as of sincerity, but as of God, in the sight of God speak we in Christ" (II Cor. 2:16, 17). Surely no better authority than this could be established, but the hazard of our ministry continues. It is often a tossing to the winds, a paddling about in sloppy weather to perform a necessity that is inconvenient, and becomes a wrestling match with tough, obdurate, resistant minds and wills. Therefore, we need the utmost in preparation and a truthful recognition of our struggle.

The illustrative concept enters to help us in the initial

stages of this undertaking. Our first aim is *attention*. There is an old theory that we must win a hearing for the gospel. It must not only be won, it must be kept. The audience that warms to a speaker at one moment may as easily cool and freeze. Sculpturing in ice is a neat trick for banquets, but it presents some miserable moments when the ice is human hearts and you're not warm enough to melt them nor sharp enough to whittle them into a swan or an angel.

Of course, there are several methods of getting attention. Humor. Antics. Shouting. Pouring milk into a hat and taking out a rabbit. Pouring milk into a hat and taking out a sloppy mess. I have come to bank largely on illustrations. I like the interest they accumulate.

An illustration is a basic, identifiable, everyday idea in which a listener may find himself related to the p/t and to the message. The hinges on this door may squeak and the panels may be paintless, but it is still a door. It may be elaborated into an ornamental monstrosity or a gorgeously decorated conversation piece; but if it is a well-hung door, a child's hand or a trembling old man may open it.

An illustration is a piece of life, a setting so familiar to the hearer, so totally believable, that a minimum of description enables him to see it and live it. Prod his memory or his consciousness, and he is in the picture, not just a spectator. If the illustration is well proportioned, well designed, well chosen, the hearer realizes that he has seen, heard, handled, felt, or experienced something identical to what the p/t is describing. This piece of common cloth has a texture the listener cannot doubt. He is a believer—at least, he is a believer in this. A level of faith must be established for the miraculous transaction: "Faith cometh by hearing, and hearing by the word of God" (Rom. 10:17). The miracle edge is in this. It is of God to perform the miracle, but God uses human instruments. One of those uses is to gain attention for the Word of God.

"The importance of the illustration for the purpose of enforcing truth is so obvious, that it seems a work of supererogation to say one word concerning it. . . . A man may often find materials to enliven a discourse which might otherwise prove very dull, or to fasten on the conscience a truth or a warning, which otherwise would have fallen on the ear unnoticed, and glided past the mind unfelt. It is not enough that truth be pointed, like a straight smooth piece of steel; it needs side points as a dart, that it may not draw out, when it effects an entrance. Anecdotes and illustrations may not only illustrate a point, and make an audience see and feel the argument, but they may themselves add to the argument; they may at once be a part of the reasoning, and an elucidation of it. Indeed, a just figure always adds power to a chain of logic, and increases the amount of truth conveyed. It is also of great use in relieving the attention, as a stopping place where the mind is rested, and prepared to resume the reasoning without fatigue, without loss. Almost any expedient, which decorum permits, may be justified, in order to awake and fix the attention of an audience. Such attention, however, cannot be *kept* but by truth worth illustrating"[3] (Cheever).

This is the appropriate point at which to distinguish that this is not a discussion of stories or how to tell stories. A story may be an illustration, but I am particularly interested in the illustration as a device by which the p/t makes the application. Stories are often self-contained units of truth and application.

Stories may be exciting, dramatic, powerful, and effective; but the story depends on many skills which are not in

---

[3]R. A. Bertram, *A Homiletic Encyclopaedia of Illustration*, (London: R. D. Dickinson, 1879).

the kit of the average p/t. This is not intended to discourage story telling nor disparage story tellers; but this is intended to encourage those who have found that costlier art beyond their capacity, to tackle the comparatively easy-to-handle illustration.

Stories are labored with a double liability: first, believability; second, acceptability through the art of the teller.

Children accept and believe a story without much question, for a good deal of their thought world and learning world necessarily includes fantasy. Older young people and adults are crusted with a sophistication that makes stories more demanding in both content and performance. It is necessary in a story to introduce characters, describe circumstances, and explain motivations. The people, situations, crises, and stimulations in the story may be foreign to the listener. He would not behave, and he cannot imagine himself behaving, as the story insinuates people behave. He may enjoy it, be amused by it, be moved to tears by it, but have no empathy with the characters presented. He toys with the suspicion that it is just a story, a fabrication, an exaggeration of half-truths strung together in a tiger-tail.

Literature and drama can afford that luxury. The ministry of the gospel cannot. The attention must be centered on something believable as a starting point to provoke faith in God.

Paul's personal testimony was a masterpiece in this arena. His record was well known. He was evidently a Jew. His history glared in his features and mannerisms. His presence, his identity with Jesus Christ, and his witness to his faith were cognizable commodities. The illustration was on its feet in front of the audience. No stretch of the imagination was required to comprehend that something had happened to this man.

Personal testimony does have limitations. Paul moved from group to group, and used it everywhere but on Mars' Hill. (That's probably why the Mars' Hill sermon is judged as his weakest.) If a testimony is used repetitively to the same group, however, the testifier will be accused of self-glorification or emptiness of new material.

Paul's writings abound with illustrations in figures: soldier, farmer, wrestler, runner, builder. Luther said, speaking of Paul, "His words are not dead words; they are living creatures with hands and feet."

"Never Man Spake Like This Man" was the title of a lecture delivered by Rev. Hugh Stowell, M.A., to the Young Men's Christian Association in Exeter Hall, on December 9, 1851. This magnificent address on the uniqueness of Jesus should be reprinted for every seminary library. Follow some of the paragraphs:

"Nothing can exceed the naturalness which Christ delighted to adopt in His gracious ministrations. He taught, not like the stilted philosophers of Greece and Rome, in abstract form and philosophic style; he loved to clothe his thoughts of matchless grandeur in the living guise which nature furnished, and to interweave them with the affections and incidents of ordinary life. Alike the Author of nature and of grace, he loved to make creation illustrate and expound revelation, and revelation throw a fresh lustre and loveliness over the face of creation. Thus he continually borrowed from the scenes and objects around him. . . . When he would represent himself in his mystical union with his church, the root of all its vitality, the spring of all its fruitfulness, he said, as he passed along to the garden of agony, 'I am the true vine, and my Father is the husbandman. Every branch in me that beareth not fruit he taketh away: and every branch that beareth fruit, he purgeth it, that it may bring forth more fruit. . . . I am the vine, ye are the branches.' . . . And need we remind you that his parables were all of them drawn from such scenes and objects as that the commonest people could most readily understand them? The shepherd with his flock, the fisherman with his net, the husbandman and his vine, the sower going forth to sow his seed, the reaper thrusting his sickle into the harvest, the woman searching for the lost piece of money—these are the artless images taken from every day life, which the Lord employed to symbolize his lessons of eternal wisdom. Such, and so familiar, from the lip Divine, was, to the beautiful definition of a parable, attributed to a child, 'the earthly story with a heavenly meaning'."

Undeniably, some great preachers and teachers have been great story tellers. Excellence in this field requires a delicate sense of timing, an ability to handle dialogue, and a descriptive ability much better developed than is needed for close-at-hand illustrations. A proficiency with dialects or a flexible voice are tremendous assets in story telling, This art is much more exacting today than twenty-five years ago. The average person has not only been exposed to literature, but he is acquainted with dramatic skills via radio and television, even if not by other dramatic media. Inasmuch as we are particularly concerned about reaching the non-Christian, we must recognize that that individual is probably well educated in the productions and skills of the entertainment world; and he does not judge us on the level of the flannelgraph nor have a Christian bias toward biblical truth. He is keenly aware of news reporting as an art by which facts, truth, half-truth, and fully outfitted rumors can be colored, bent, and applied to the desire of the report, the prejudice of the agency, or the policy of politics. Acquaintance with the informed and entertained world makes such a listener resistant to any dramatic effort which is less than professional. Stories are wonderful implements to melt hearts and present the claims of Christ, but demands on both teller and hearer are much greater than in the use of an everyday happening which illustrates a spiritual truth. This avenue is always open to the hearer's faith. He must receive the illustration because he knows it is true regardless of the skill of the p/t.

HOW YOU GET THAT WAY

CHAPTER TWO

HOW YOU GET THAT WAY

The illustrative concept is a way of looking at things. In fact, it is a way of looking and looking and looking at everything. It examines the texture of every fabric, missing not a color and neglecting not a thread. It examines the tangible and intangible for the substance of an illustration. It talks and questions, queries and probes, suspects and haunts each facet and fact, each foible and fancy which comes under its observation. It milks secrets out of stone and wraps warm imagination around the aggravating tone of a squeaking shoe. Nothing is too small to excite it. Nothing is large enough to discourage it from toying with the fringe of the robe and hoping for the touch of inspiration.

The illustrative concept requires conscious effort. You may lose some pleasures which you formerly enjoyed, in order to use the landscape instead of just stare at it.

I was an ardent camera buff, lugging equipment in an outsize pouch that hung about me like a pregnant kangaroo. I got some pictures. I also lost the pleasure of the moment. I was too busy squinting through the range-finder to see anything but the picture. I resigned the camera for a more exhausting art. Now I concentrate on every shadow and scene, framing the moment as an illustration to put a door into some message. I am so thoroughly oriented to this preferred watching that I often lose what others enjoy in attempting to make an image of memory become a teacher of truth.

This way of looking at things does not happen suddenly. Unlike photography, you cannot buy a lot of equipment and—after a cursory acquaintance with the camera and meter—produce fairly satisfactory pictures. If the illustrative concept is a way of looking at things, it has a prerequisite in a way of thinking of things. There is a philosophy in Romans 1 concerning God's revelation of Himself to men. We understand that man by wisdom knows not God, and the saving revelation resides exclusively in that blessed Redeemer; but a logical premise exists for finding God's handiwork, God's formats, God's truth, in everything that is; for He has made everything. Things are what they are because that is the way He made them. Sin has perverted what God made, but a basic truth concerning God underlies all creation, shines through all of nature, is encountered in the experiences of life, and is even evidenced in the manufacture of men. Obviously a man can do what he does with materials because this is the way God made and ordained things. No violation of God's creative prerogatives or providential government is insinuated by science, invention, or the events of life.

Therefore, because God is truth and truthful, anything or everything can bring us back to some lesson God wants to teach. All of time and experience contain information

He wants to impart or the gospel He desires to have heard. As a minister of God's truth I am handed a big box filled with all the varieties of matter, sensation, and intelligence; and I am told to use these pieces as they fit into harmony with the will and the Word of God. This way of thinking leads to this way of looking at all of life and life's predicaments and pleasures.

This way of looking does have its frustrations.

There are good days. You run into a ripe orchard, where fruits hang thick and juicy from every limb. But the next day you are lost in a forest where every branch is bare. A few scrawny fruits you think you see dissolve into fiddle-faddle when you try to pluck them.

Cherish the days when you find the abundance.

A storage system is obligatory. The jotting of many notes can become a weariness, and sorting them from quixotic scratchings into indexed beauty is an onerous task. But it is highly rewarding. The busy p/t has endless demand for this material. He is always using it. The remuneration for good material is the increasing demand for more and better material. Faithful care of ten pounds results in the burden of ten cities. Good work does not bring freedom from work. It brings a greater need for discrimination and more work.

The illustrative concept becomes a reexamination of each property every time you travel across it. Nothing is discarded simply because it is familiar. Thousands of people have looked upon a block of marble and rejected it. But the sculptor saw a statue in it. He also had the skill to get the statue out of the stone or, perhaps more accurately, to cut away the stone from the statue. The artist must be efficient at both points: he must be able to see the statue and he must be able to produce it.

Nothing guarantees that once you see the illustration you will be able to make others see it. We will examine later some of the tools for this process, but I must concede that there are many failures in the attempt to hang a door where a door should be. It is disillusioning and humiliating to watch what you thought was a perfect illustration dissolve into triviality, with your listeners asking each other through their curtained eyes, "What was he trying to say?"

As a small boy of six or seven years I could see a horse in a cake of soap. Lots of kids and parents were cutting things out of cakes of soap. They sliced angels from Fels-Naphtha, yellow cats from Jap Rose, and green old men with a schoolgirl's complexion from Palmolive. I have always been clumsy with my hands, but I was determined to stab forth an orange horse from Lifebuoy. I managed a crude outline, but I amputated a leg with a sudden gash. I tried to salvage a wagon out of it, but lost a wheel. I wound up with a snake—a very short, straight snake with no rattles.

I have experienced the same frustration in having an illustration wear out to suds in my sweaty palms. The instantaneous glimpse of elucidation went bicycling off in the wind into bubbles when I attempted to turn it into a visible form. It is very likely that what I saw was real enough, but I just could not make it appear without whittling it away. A good vignette is often ruined by a poor craftsman. Another consideration is that some of the greatest images you obtain will not illustrate anything— that is, not anything you have under appointment. That is why a treasure chest is necessary. An event, a sight, a drama in the street, a patch of wallpaper from some room—all these may deeply move you. At that precise moment you may be too close to the actuality to be able to translate it to others. But hang onto it! It may become your finest piece of communication a year from now.

Admittedly, some moments must be captured at the instant of happening or they lose relevance. But that is the exceptional item. The drama can be lived again if you keep it alive in your heart. Notice how many historical moments continue their excitement, perhaps even accelerate in excitement, by the passing of time. The assassination of President Kennedy, the Hitlerian slaughter of the Jews, and the papers of Winston Churchill during the war years become actually more relevant now than when the events occurred.

There is an idle hope cherished by many inexperienced speakers. They imagine the more experienced avoid the work, and that their own reward for more experience will be the ability to make ideas come alive in the pressure of the moment. But this is not a sensible dream. The reality is that you must see the figure clearly, and you must have a precise plan for making others see it. The only torment worse than having others wonder what you were trying to say, is to be uncertain yourself as to what you were trying to say.

I have devised another three-point landing gear for my own convenience in finding, using, and making profitable the illustrative quality I am continually stumbling over, brushing against, and living through.

A. Isolation

B. Identification

C. Interpretation

Each of these is necessary, and each must be well executed at its own point in the process to make the door operate efficiently. The doormaker should be careful that preliminary work is completed before the guests arrive. Tours of inspection are not very satisfactory when you have to warn the spectators to be careful of the tools on the floor or to, please, disregard the unfinished work which is hidden behind the paint-splattered canvas. It is hard to find many things more infuriating and disconcerting than a door that only opens a few inches because it doesn't clear the carpet or a door that dances into your arms because the pins weren't put into the hinges. No one can predict all the possibilities of failure, but the obvious causes should be eliminated before they have a chance to chagrin you in public.

ISOLATION

CHAPTER THREE

ISOLATION

The proverbial query about the precedence of the chicken or the egg has been compounded into sharps and flats for the musical arena: which comes first, the words or the music? The three possible answers all receive a vote or two from the experts in the field, for experience parades back and forth among the contestants, now giving the nod to the lyrics, now to the melody, and at last confusing the spectators by a tie. Therefore, take your choice:

1. The music
2. The words
3. Both together, at the same time, because they are part of each other

If we push the same question in the homiletic field we will get the same answers. And so, which comes first, the illustration or the application? Probably the most frequent answer would be that they sprouted forth together, and that if Esau preceded Jacob, he knew he was being followed by Jacob's hand on his heel. This might be more a result of our faulty memories, however, than the actual fact. Illustrations do not come forth on call like a dog at a whistle. If they do answer the whistle, it's because you've owned them for a long time and have them trained. It is unbelievable that a p/t suddenly confronts an idea and asks, "How can I illustrate this?" The conscious inquiry might indicate he is an index-hound who has a file on Atonement, Bible, Cross, and Death. Probably he has catalogued the distillation of heaven's dew on others' property: Love—Vol. 129.5, page 16, paragraph 3. This is a legitimate and workable method which has been highly successful for thousands. All of us, at one time or another, in the beginning of our ministry or under severe pressure of time, have used canned illustrations. The extravagant use of time, however, which is necessary to file, index, and learn how to use such systems, could be more profitably spent in isolating material which is your own. This will give freshness, clarity, and the joy of creativity to the task.

The illustrative concept begins with the recognition that every truth we handle is staring at us wherever we look, and the illustrations of it are as plentiful as we have eyes to see and ears to hear. This way of thinking, of looking at things, begins by isolating events, words, experiences, and ideas, so that we are continuously making our own catalog of illustrative material by the very process of living. This will revolutionize your attitude toward people and incidents. You do not go anywhere as a tourist to be entertained, but every adventure of day and night is as a merchant seeking goods to sell and customers to buy. The obvious paraphrase of the scriptural injunction is, "He that hath a mind to think, let him think; he that hath a memory to fill, let him fill it."

" 'Where shall I gather illustrations for my class?' On

this source from which they are drawn depends, in a great measure, their value. Good bank-notes come from the banker, not from the counterfeiter. No one has any right to have counterfeits, so no teacher has a right to use spurious illustrations. Convey the truth by the simplest illustrations possible, and with the least circumlocution. . . . Go into the streets with open eyes. . . . Be wide awake, be discriminating; or, if the expression may be allowed, possess sanctified gumption" (R. A. Bertram).

Some of what you see, hear, think, and feel will be lost, even if you keep elaborate notes and take scads of pictures. There is a diminution of the importance and relevance of some particulars which appear pertinent at the moment and place of occurrence. Souvenir pillows inscribed gaudily, "From the little shop under the big pines," are to be found in basements, closets, car trunks, and by fireplaces; and their sole destiny seems to be to prompt the question, "Why did you insist on buying that monstrosity?" Necessarily, there is an overgathering of material, some of which will make you wonder why you ever thought it important.

Memory all alone is a wobbly stem, however; and the heavy flower heads may snap it off in a gentle wind. It is amusing to read Mr. Bertram's ninety-year-old advice: "Let the copyist write only on one side of the page. Paper is cheap, and a neglect of this counsel will lead to many inconveniences and regrets." Good advice when writing scripts, but for memory propping use anything at hand. Now that memo pads come complete with your printed name and address by buying a dozen four-color pens or a crate of ballpoints, and pocket secretaries are awarded for merely trying out a color TV or inquiring about the cost of insurance on the family goldfish, no one should be without a paper and pen. But I always am. I borrow pencils from waiters to scratch ridiculous lines on paper napkins. I also have to decipher notes from the glue side of S and H stamps, the edges of gasoline charge cards, and the inside of gum wrappers. I tried once to write some notes on butter, as advocated by some pen manufacturer, only to discover I had a greasy pocket and the whole idea melted. I also had a hard time explaining the blue lines on the toast the next morning.

Although memory nods—and sometimes break—under a heavy load, it is nonetheless a miracle healer. A small reminder, a simple sketch or line, will bring back an idea with great clarity. If prompted at all, memory, like a small boy who needs only a nudge to play his whole piano repertoire or recite his whole part in the Christmas pageant, will particularize details and colors and emotions of a given setting. Perhaps years after the actual occurrence, a choice illustration will come floating in like a well-stocked ship you put to sea and forgot until it sailed home wearing your flag.

The name of the game is isolation. It is appropriating some sight or action just for itself alone. The artist and photographer do this in composing and framing a picture. The dramatist—indeed, every writer—uses the same technique in removing a moment of life from all that surrounds it, enlarging it and then framing it on a background which makes that moment important. If you see one part of a man's character as it is by itself or if you compress one era of a man's life into a moment of time or if, conversely, you exaggerate one moment into a book, the isolation becomes drama. Realistically, probably nothing is dramatic in its own context. Life includes all the prosaic elements which militate against the spectacular: getting up in the morning, shaving, drinking tea when your stomach's upset, sending out the laundry, getting a haircut, and feeding the cat. Each of these, isolated from its normal surroundings, can be made into a drama by proper framing. Obviously it is even simpler to dramatize a unique, sensational, highly emotional situation, especially when the dull, monotonous background is removed and the moment stands alone.

The illustrative way of looking at things includes this isolation strategy. You dare not look at every object and word, thinking, all the while, "What does it illustrate?" The strain will blur your vision. But you can look on each object and word with a concentration that enables you to see the moment or the action just as it is. There is a wholesome curiosity known as observation. It is specific rather than panoramic. It forgets the forest to see the tree. It can by-pass drapes, new furniture, and shining windows to talk with an old man whose cane may help you down a path to fondle a beautiful truth. This busy little imp may not compliment the hostess on a tastefully furnished home but may demand the history of a carved figure that excites the imagination. On such pretext you may obtain a personally conducted tour that will not net one idea, but you may wind up with a fistful of brilliant gems plucked from the eye-sockets of heathen idols.

The greatest value of the isolation process is that you see the illustration: it teaches you so that you can teach another. My severest criticism of the indexed illustration file is that you can use it without learning how to see the illustration. There is some virtue in a young artist copying the work of the established master. He learns color values, style, proportion, and a number of other valuable lessons. But there is one art you cannot master in being a copyist, and that is to see the picture. The magic that excites is in the ability to see. In rehearsing what someone else says, a man may illustrate an idea without teaching himself. I have read and heard many illustrations which to me were weak, incompetent, and far from the point. I am willing to grant, however, that the man who used it saw the point and received more from it than he was able to communicate to me or than I was able to receive, in which case the illustration was valid. But if neither of us got anything out of it, it was a failure. I have heard p/t's use illustrations which were conspicuously borrowed, which I am sure they did not comprehend for themselves but were thrown to the listeners in the vague hope that that which the speaker could not digest might, nevertheless, feed some hungry soul. I felt like a seal being thrown a nickel's worth of food from a slot machine, which the benefactor would not consider swallowing himself but which he hoped the seal would find tasty. I didn't.

While serving as pastor of Calvary Church, Grand Rapids, Michigan, the congregation bit off a building program that including swallowing a mortgage and praying to digest it with liberal doses of alkaline offering plates. It was my first experience with building anything—church, house, or chicken coop. I was determined to find some well-constructed illustrations among the hammers and power saws. Church officialdom included some experienced builders to hold daily consultation over progress with a keen eye for satisfactory material and workmanship. The architect was alert and fastidious. I expected to learn by asking questions, but discovered my questions did not provoke intelligent answers. I suspected that if I were other than the minister they would have laughed at my naivete. As it was, I was stared at with the unvoiced inquiry: "How long has it been since your breakdown?"

The whole noisy, dusty, maddeningly slow operation was disillusioning. I had dreamt that it would go up like Solomon's Temple: every piece perfectly fitted together to spare the muss, fuss, and cuss that rumbled under some breaths when I happened by. It was particularly distressing to find so much clean-up necessary. Every night a few minutes were given to sweeping scraps, sawdust, and pebbles of concrete into little piles that floated forth over the whole place the next day. Week-ends banged down the lids on tool chests, piled up lumber in stacks, with plastic-shrouded bags, bricks, and boxes of ceiling tile, until it looked more like the viewing room for the remains of the dead than the nursery of a new facility.

Then I saw the broken window.

I was aghast!

It had an unpainted frame, and it had been shattered before the painters had even touched it. Then there were broken tiles in the floor before a scuff mark was on them. The plumbing fixtures were chipped before hot and cold ran through them. There were myriad tiny defects that had to be patched, mended, reset again, glued, reglued, brushed over, placed, and replaced before the building was completed.

There was one fact I isolated from the building business: new buildings need repair. This became a usable illustration that a newborn child of God may need repair. Older Christians forget this. They expect perfect conduct from young Christians to match their perfect standing in Christ. But this is not realistic. New cars must be serviced. Babies need shots, surgery, and seventy-times-seven changes. New buildings need repair before they are fit for occupancy.

Ordinarily isolating one illustration starts the parade. One after another keeps falling into the line of march by the phenomenon of association. This is especially present in a peculiarly human situation which almost everyone encounters. The eye, the ear, the mind—all must be narrowed down to one detail: in this case, the broken window, the cracked tile, the splintered board.

The isolation policy also applies to conversation. You are bombarded with opinions, anecdotes, bright sayings of children, amusing and tragic recitals, and commercials that are living bah. You are seeking for one line, one sentence, one shining word in that truckload of dialogue. If this makes you feel like a garbage picker, join the union; good silverware is sometimes found in the garbage. Not often do people tell you the best or the worst about themselves. This is saved for those they love or those they fear, and you ordinarily hear what will make them appear as part of the common scene. Be wary of everything you hear, but keep listening for the angel song. Shepherds and Judean nights are not for the privileged few alone. Daniel heard it while the lions growled, and Peter woke up to it in jail.

J-One and J-Two are cousins. At six years each they have passed through the stages of good, bad, and never indifferent. Both are girls, and their mothers have found it convenient to use each other as baby-sitters on appropriate occasions. The two Js have played together a great deal more than cousins who meet only at family reunions.

Following an afternoon of the two Js together, the mother of J-Two was putting her to bed at night. J-Two is the quiet one who follows whatever J-One recommends. Now J-Two had a dirty face, dirty neck, and dirty hands. Her mother was horrified at the extent and depth of the dirt. She remembered distinctly telling both girls to wash up for dinner. The condition suggested that her instructions had not been followed.

"Didn't you wash up for dinner like I told you?"

"Oh, yes," said J-Two.

"Well, it surely doesn't look like it. Now, I know you both went into the bathroom. Did you use soap and water and a wash rag?"

Detailed probing scored with a confession. True, the two Js had trotted into the bathroom. Then J-One had proposed the plan to beat the rap.

"Just run the water," she said, "and they'll think we're washing."

It would be impossible to list, remember, and use all the cute things said or done by children. Art Linkletter compiles them into books, but thousands of such stories are being carted around in the minds of parents, grandparents, aunts, uncles, and Mr. Weaver who lives next door to Dennis. The p/t, however, is sensitive to one type of report. He is not uniquely interested in children's psychological maneuverings of their parents. He is listening for one clear, illuminating, penetrating concept that he can cut away from all that surrounds it, so that the illustration will be plainly seen by everyone, including himself.

Notice that J-One's philosophy is a perfect hook on which to hang the whole case for a pretense of religion: "Just run the water. . . ." The ceremonial observance, the creedal confession, the ritualistic performance, the orthodox position, the head nodding and aisle walking—all are equated in running the water but not washing the hands. These are gimmicks that adults use to make other adults think they are religious or spiritual. I presume they imagine God can be deceived the same way. This opens the door to enforce the necessity of right relationship with God through faith in Jesus Christ. There is no inference that there is anything criminal about running the water, but it is hypocritical to use the sound of obedience to indicate a fulfillment of obedience.

Personal reading always has been the richest source of illustrative perception. Reading and filing illustrations can be, as I have already insinuated, about as exciting as making sandwiches with bakery bread. Reading informative, stimulating, classic, scientific, or imaginative authors, however, will open rich areas of material never found in books of static illustrations. Ruskin is a jungle of ideas. You may have to carve them out delicately and carry them piggy-back, being careful not to damage them on the trees in the way. It's not easy going to get to them either. This is apparent in that out of all of Ruskin's voluminous portfolios, only one item is frequently quoted in illustration books. It is a beautiful little piece about the dirt on the workmen's path which is composed of sand, clay, water, and soot.

Ruskin folded the application right into his observation like a chocolate chip in a cookie of the same name. He noted that each of these elements, separated from the others and allowed to follow its natural course under right conditions, became something far removed from mud. The clay would become a sapphire, the sand an opal, the soot carbon or diamond, and the water rain, dew, or snow.

Ruskin is a pirate's chest of such sparklers if you have the patience to do deep-sea diving and roaming around in heavily wooded coves.

Most p/t's have discovered Shakespeare for themselves or have been introduced by a professional writer of illustrations, although a great many speakers tremble to borrow from this source. There are several hazards. Quotations from Shakespeare must be letter perfect or some former performer in *A Midsummer Night's Dream* will wrestle you for a comma. To make a point with William's spear you must often describe the setting and interpret the Elizabethan English of the Bard of Avon. By the time you get through, the Avon lady has rung the bell.

It would be a serious mistake to assume that only old authors are peddlers of such goods. New authors not only incorporate usable ideas, but they update one's jargon and word values. This does not mean that writers of fiction or history or drama will hand you ready-made illustrations. They often allow the truth to lie between the lines, as a farmer cuts an irrigation ditch through the fields to carry water to the crops.

Technical magazines and trade journals usually contain some eminently useful material. The great advantage in keeping up with these publications is that your illustration is not only contemporary but accurate. Scientific illustrations (especially in the medical field) may be useful but run the peril of inaccuracy due to the rapid expansion of knowledge in such areas. Well-informed people may be disenchanted by the use of faulty material. This fact alone keeps a p/t in constant research; for an idea presented with the best intentions, and previously with good effect, may backfire if the listener discovers your information is not current.

A church has a responsibility to supply both its teachers and members with resource books, helpful study aids, commentaries, Christian fiction, and the other publications related to Christian life and ministry. No church library, however, could be expected to provide the amount of material which is available in any good public library. If you begin bringing illustrations from areas far afield from the norm of pulpits and Sunday schools, you will find it so exhilarating you will want to increase this adventure. Such material stiffens your spine and gives listeners a heads-up attitude. *The Readers' Guide to Periodical Literature* is the most valuable of all research books. Its index of subjects and authors in every leading publication is a highway to mountainsides of wild and beautiful exposures of truth. The one problem will be to cut the landscape to size and cart it home in your wheelbarrow.

Samuel Eliot Morison's imposing volume, *The Oxford History of the American People,* accommodates one sentence which made it worthwhile to navigate the 1,122 pages. Delineating attitudes during the Civil War, Morison writes, "By May 1861 everyone had taken his stand . . . there was no switching sides . . . no defection, but plenty of desertion by soldiers of both sides."

This statement could be quickly cut away from its surroundings. It takes only a few seconds to describe what it refers to. In a flash you could move right into the present spiritual condition when many Christians desert, although they do not defect. Multitudes of believers believe what they have believed for years. They have not changed their concept of how to be saved or their definition of regeneration. When pushed to it, they give a pretty good testimony. They are not thieves, murderers, adulterers, cheats, alcoholics, or child beaters. They are honest citizens, solid and respectable. But they have deserted.

They have deserted the church, except for a once-a-week or less attendance. Their program of Christianity is convenient, but not constraining. The soldier has gone back to farming or blacksmithing while the war rages on at the front. He is satisfied with earning a living instead of a medal. He is content with shiny, well-heeled shoes on a temporary street rather than eternal treasures in the city foursquare.

In this chapter I have isolated three illustrations. A great deal of irrelevant material—at least, irrelevant to the ultimate application—has to be cut away. Notice them in order.

A. One idea from the building program: new buildings need repair. This item was found by personal observation.

B. The scheme of the children to fool the adults: "Just run the water. . . ." This was isolated by listening to ordinary conversation.

C. The present-day description of some Christians from a line from Samuel Eliot Morison's *The Oxford History of the American People.* This idea was found in contemporary literature.

In each of these the application is almost automatic, and it would be difficult to say whether the illustration or the application came first. In a later chapter I will discuss interpretation from a different side of the problem. Ordinarily a basic application comes with the moment of isolation. How to code, index, and satisfactorily file such material with all its potentials is almost an impossibility until the material has been written somewhat extensively, given a public hearing, and simmered a bit on the low burner. Much isolated material may float around on odd bits of paper or be dumped into a folder marked "Ideas" until it is actually put to use. Ordinarily, however, these scraps do not long remain orphans without a name.

IDENTIFICATION

CHAPTER FOUR

IDENTIFICATION

Identification encompasses all the mechanical skills by which the p/t will enable the hearer to enter into the illustration. This is where and how we hang the door.

I must reemphasize the necessity to see your own illustration, to fully comprehend and mentally identify it. This is not the place to attempt instrument flying. Blessed is the p/t who gets the point himself, for verily I say unto you he will sharpen it as he gives it to others. Whether you are relating what you have seen, heard, read, or experienced, the whole concept must be clear in your mind before it can be translated to a listener. We have enough difficulty hauling our ideas to market on the rude vehicle of words without struggling with nondescript boxes, unlabeled and coming apart at the seams, which we hope to mend in the process of transporting them from the dim shadows of our consciousness into the bright light of public inspection. If it appears this detail is being labored unduly, a few panic-producing expeditions or listener-chilling, palm-sweating, throat-drying, mind-numbing moments will convince one that too much preparation is about as impossible as too much underwear in 50 below zero weather.

There are only so many methods of preparation of spoken material. Most experienced speakers have tried them all and settled on one. T. DeWitt Talmage has a hilarious sketch about his first attempt at preaching without notes. Many masters of pulpit and classroom have written or told about their method of preparation and why they used it. Most of them have confided their experiences of trying other methods after years of certain practices. Ordinarily the adventurer has returned, sometimes screaming, to his old ways, A few, such as Talmage, weathered the shocking and horrendous incident of a novel delivery, and resolved to overcome their fears and open a new era of ministry.

This is not a book of homiletics, per se, but some basic consideration of methods of preparation and delivery is appropriate to the general area of illustrative material. A few variations may squeeze between the lines, but standard procedures come in the following categories:

1. Fully written material which is carried into the pulpit and read
2. Fully written material which is studied, outlined, and the outline carried into the pulpit
3. Fully written material which is memorized
4. Partially written material of which an elaborate outline is made, important passages written fully, and the whole memorized
5. An outline written and carried into the pulpit
6. Extemporaneous preaching of two types:

a. Message outlined, but preached as the form takes shape in the pulpit

b. Message totally developed in mind and heart, preached fully as it takes shape in the pulpit

(There is a style called spontaneous which only an idiot would attempt, unless called on in some emergency. Even in emergency a p/t should have some sort of preparation which he can quickly rally to his help. Spontaneous indicates total unpreparedness, a vaulting into the occasion and saying whatever comes to mind without previous thought or arrangement. This is inherently unscriptural, for we are told to "study to show thyself approved unto God, a workman that needeth not to be ashamed, rightly dividing the word of truth" [II Tim. 2:15]. This method would be impossible in an enduring ministry, for it would result in constant repetition or ridiculous ranting.)

Two explanatory notes are important.

First, memorization varies according to the memorizer. Some men given to this style are so bound by their memory that they cannot deviate one word from the preestablished pattern. I heard a great preacher confess publicly that he memorized every word and if someone stopped him in the middle, he didn't know what he'd do. Most memorizers are not so encumbered. They can extemporize and do so frequently, so that their memories serve them rather than they serving their memories.

Ancient orators were generally memorizers, and in this method many great English preachers followed. The German and French pulpits also highly favored it. J. M. Hoppin, who dedicates his volume on homiletics to his old teacher, Dr. August Neander, states bluntly: "Robert Hall, it is well known, mingled the extemporaneous and memoriter methods; and on most occasions made use of his memory for the delivery of the most important and finished parts of his sermon. The following is related of him:

" 'Once in a conversation with a few friends who had led him to talk of his preaching, and to answer, among other questions, one respecting the supposed and reported extemporaneous production of the most striking parts of his sermons, in the earlier period of his ministry, he surprised us by saying the most of them, so far from being extemporaneous, had been so deliberately prepared that his words were selected, and the construction and order of the sentences adjusted.!' "[4]

Second, extemporaneous preaching is usually considered the highest form of the public-speaking art. It is surely the most demanding. Rather than requiring less preparation it actually takes more. It is the most nerve-shattering device if you hit a dry spell—and everyone does, you know. It has been mastered by few men, and it is not recommended for the novice. I am convinced that those who have become extemporaneous speakers over a long period of time have attained this by means of the easier methods and were equipped in experience and material to negotiate the hazards of this undertaking which could easily turn into your own funeral.

Regardless of how the material is eventually used in actual delivery—read, memorized, or outlined—I want to enter a strong plea for fully writing out illustrations, especially for their first employment. Illustrations lifted from books, indices, and so forth, are written for you, but should be rewritten by the person who intends to use them. But a new illustration which you have isolated for your use should be written carefully if you hope to have the listener identify with it and with you. This should be a

---

[4] Foster's "Essay on Robert Hall," in *Homiletics,* By James M. Hoppin, (New York: Funk and Wagnalls, 1883).

standard procedure for every p/t for the first twenty years at least, and by then he won't be able to do less. This should apply to every illustration, dug roots and all from the common soil or clipped from a neighbor's hedge, loaded with fruit or decorated with ornaments and tinsel.

Nothing so sets a pattern, so firms up an application, so deliberately isolates the important from the meaningless, as writing, rewriting, and then writing again. I cannot be too emphatic in urging young men in the early years of their ministry or anyone trying to improve his presentation of truth to write—write what you think, see, feel. Then write it again. This is the costly investment, but it pays dividends. The discriminating p/t will find the cheap items are shopworn, frail, and unreliable. Usually someone else tried them on for size and found them disillusioning. The expensive investment not only is the best investment, but an actual saving of time and effort in future years.

Of course, there are some people fluent in language. It is imagined that this art pops up like a wart. But fluency is an earned gift. The fluent man is fluent with words he has heard, read, or laboriously dug from a dictionary or thesaurus. He does not simply make sounds—he says words, words that make sense. Ordinarily this indicates an investment in writing. A few people are speakers without being writers, but they are not capable speakers without work.

When you have written the illustration, read it over as you would read someone else's effort. This is difficult to do, because you read it as you think it, not just as you would read unfamiliar material. But does it say what you saw? what you heard? what you felt? Will the person who listens to you see what you saw, heard, felt? Will the listener identify himself with you and walk through the door with you?

It is thoroughly appropriate and wise to ask someone to read it or to listen to you read it. And do not ask that person if it is good. Ask him if he sees the picture. Ask him if the point is clear.

Admittedly there is an extra dimension when the words are spoken. The capable p/t has the advantage of facial expressions, gestures, emphasis by raising or lowering the voice, and a multitude of other tricks to make the picture complete. Therefore, if the written product has cohesion and clarity so that a reader can identify the action or emotions of the setting, the spoken version should be stronger. An illustration can crumble to nothing, however, becoming either a total misfit, a scab on the scenery, or a hesitating pedestrian uncertain if to wait on the curb or cross the street, because no absolute definition was made by the p/t in his preparation. He could not decide what he saw, what he intended to say, nor how he expected to say it.

This is a common error of people who attempt to tell you what they read in a book or what they heard someone say. They grope for words because they do not see the picture inside their mind. They probably read without really comprehending or they heard without hearing, retaining simply a vague notion that it was very good if they could just think of it. The original fault may be traceable to the source from which they are attempting to borrow; but it is frustrating when a conversation bumbles on to a muttered, "Well, it was something like that anyhow."

Obviously, years of practice and experience shorten the demands of written preparation, except that such experience demands higher and more exacting standards. If progress does not completely eliminate the work, it does spare the drudgery of the same mistakes. A concert artist never reaches a point where he can keep his skill at peak level with less practice, but one presumes that with the years he practices with more proficiency and pleasure.

A few decisions necessarily precede even the writing of an illustration. If it is personal in any element there is merit in relating it from that angle. The personal involvement adds authority immediately, which is especially useful when the p/t has acceptance by his listeners.

The first person factor does have some complications. There is a temptation to use material heard or read in the first person, and then comes the old question, "Is this legitimate? Is it poetic license to borrow an idea and tell it as though it happened to you?" It is simpler, for it removes the necessity to keep repeating, "he said, he did, he thought." It makes the illustration much warmer and more effective.

The question of legitimacy is using others' ideas as your own is sticky because it is so commonly practiced. It is interesting to read old books and discover how illustrations went from generation to generation, from town to town, from one theological camp to another, and somehow managed to happen to each one who told them. This liberty has been taken by the least and the greatest. Some organization could make a fortune by issuing certificates granting permission to use pilfered material without giving credit for the source.

Lest this chapter fall into the hands of some unknowing or misunderstanding reader, it is appropriate to include a few paragraphs about plagiarism.

In the Homiletic Review of 1880 there is a quotation from a book which quotes from *Tristam Shandy* about

Yorick, a minister, who carefully noted date and place of each of his sermons, usually including a comment about it. On one Yorick recorded: "For this sermon I shall be hanged—for I have stolen the greater part of it. Dr. Paidagunes found me out." Therefore, if long and common practice sanctifies a craft, however dishonest, this ancient art is ready for sainthood.

Every public speaker—or nonpublic speaker for that matter—consciously or unconsciously borrows material. The one possible exception would be a specialist who has done new research in some field; but even he must necessarily use accumulated information which made possible whatever new work he accomplished. Indeed, this is one reason for publishing books, especially study books and other volumes which will be helpful for those who teach others. Sermons, lectures, Bible studies, and ordinary conversations would be a series of quotes, footnotes, and credit lines if every idea not original with the speaker had to be precisely and specifically acknowledged. A person gathers thoughts, ideas, and illustrations, and then puts them through his own process of construction and application.

I understand this.

It is comparable to many manufactured products. The automobile may be built by General Motors with body by Fisher, steel by Republic, tires by U.S. Rubber, vinyl by LaFrance, plastics by Dow, and cigarette lighter by I-Don't-Care-if-You-Do-Get-Cancer. I accept this as legitimate, and I know what they mean when they sell the car as a Chevrolet, Pontiac, or Buick.

There is a similar process in the preparation of a message or a lesson which most people understand. There are times, however, when credit lines are necessary in the light of real honesty. When making direct quotation, naming the author is not only honest but may add luster to the quotation by giving it authority.

Printed illustrations are thrown into the public market to be used, but the idea of using someone's illustration as though it happened to me is out of bounds with both my purpose and my conscience.

I have learned, however, to walk cautiously here and not conclude that things cannot happen twice. Dr. E. J. Bulgin told me that his father had an experience along a country road when he picked up a traveler who was carrying a large pack on his back. The stranger, upon invitation, got into the wagon with Bulgin's father and sat quietly, still wearing the heavy load.

His benefactor said, "Why don't you take off that pack and put it back in the wagon? You'll be more comfortable."

"Oh, no," said the burdened man; "it's nice enough of you to give me a ride without haulin' my pack, too."

Dr. Bulgin told me that years later he heard this same story told by an outstanding preacher as though he, the preacher, had picked up the stranger. Bulgin added, "I am sure my father did not repeat this story in any manner that it would get to that preacher. It is perfectly possible that in a day of horses and wagons this incident could have happened twice."

I will accept that explanation. It might even have been the same traveler. Some fellows never learn.

This explanation does not always seem reasonable, however. Jeremy Taylor's sermon on death begins: "Where our kings are crowned their ancestors lie buried, and they must walk over their grandsires' heads to take their crown." This has an uncomfortable word-for-word likeness to a previously published poem by Francis Beaumont. One commentator graciously labeled this "unconscious coincidence."

When a p/t says, "The Lord gave this to me," I accept his statement. If I have read the same idea in a book or do read it a few days later, I do not doubt the p/t. God does reveal truth by His Spirit, and there is continuity in this revelation through the Word. Certain coincidences are inevitable. I recently used an illustration about grandparents showing off the pictures of their grandchildren, and half-a-dozen people said at the door, "I see you saw 'Petticoat Junction' last night." Purely by coincidence "Petticoat Junction" had used such an idea ahead of me, and anyone who knew me well would know I wouldn't come in with such an obvious theme the next day. (Next year maybe—but not the next morning.)

Exact wordings, phrases uniquely turned, and abnormal coincidence repetition—all these make the listener suspect the p/t has a dustpan memory and he should be more careful how he empties it. Some latitude is allowable in imagination, the elaboration of a point of view, and use of publicized information. Education is foundationed on the communication of ideas, demonstrated theories, recorded data, and classic examples of the best of every form of art. No one criticizes an organist for playing what Bach wrote, but it would be an offense for an organist to pretend he wrote it. The delicacy of this question, not only as related to the listener but as related to the narrator, demands that the p/t keep a sensitive conscience about the manner he uses gems from other mines. Abraham Lincoln is alleged to have said that no man has a good enough memory to make a successful liar. This does become the trap, especially if you talk about an experience in Jerusalem and then later try to raise money for your first trip to the Holy Land.

Let's assume you have isolated some idea you think is relevant to the point. You have decided in what manner to relate it—that is, in the first person or as a narrator or as defined by some other person. Try it on for size by writing it out, word for word. You may sit silently trying to find the opening sentence. The paper will stare up at you. Your hand will shake. You will pray for the phone to ring, someone to ask you to come out and play catch, or for your foot to itch so that you'd have something to scratch and take your mind off that paper. But if you have that much trouble starting the whole business while sitting all alone, imagine what a job you'd have starting this idea in front of an audience. Realistically, when faced with the necessity of saying something in front of an audience, we do; but much of the definition is lost in speaking off the top of our head, when we should be speaking from the depths of our hearts, the fulness of our minds, and the conviction of our spirits. Trying to write out your idea soon reveals what dull lines you have often used when you didn't take time to sharpen them. A hand-drawn outline, a point-by-point sketch of the general plan, will give better structure to the material. The self-probing question needs repetition: what was I trying to say?

A certain amount of description becomes necessary to enable the listener to see the door and cross the threshold with you. This does not mean poetry—just description. Some novices feel defeated before they begin because they do not have the words or the rhythm of language to sew the stars like silver buttons on the black tunic of the night in the manner of some old pro they heard. It is convenient to be fluent, and it adds a touch of color to be able to write material so that the audience hears the swish of the ocean's broom leveling out a sand castle. But this art is more hazardous than essential. Many a good illustration, like the tail of a lost kite, has been left hanging in the branches and foliage of fancy phrases. The audience is not a foursome who joins you in seeking a lost ball while you eloquently swing a club in the tall grasses of oratory.

Description, in this context, is not intended to do anything more than identify the action or the actor. Language is a magic gallery of the mind which opens easily at a gentle prod from a familiar word. Most of the usable words are picture words. It is a dull conversation when the sound track runs on and the picture lamp is dark. There is only one aim at this moment: you want your hearer to know where you are and what you see and what you feel. You are tacitly inviting him to join you. He will fill in some of the details for himself, especially if your illustration has been gleaned from a common, down-to-earth situation, in which he has often found himself.

If you drive into a city with which you are unacquainted but in which you have a friend, you may stop at a public telephone to just say hello. Your friend, however, insists that you come out to the house for dinner or he may suggest coming right down to where you are for a cup of coffee. In almost any such situation you will have to identify your location. This does not require extraordinary use of language or unfamiliar words. If within sight of street signs, you may say, "Let's see, I'm at Third Street; and it looks like the cross street is—Han—Hanover."

But even if you have no such advantage, you won't panic and shout, "I can't tell you where I am." You will probably begin a simple description. "There's a tall building on the corner. Five—eight—twelve stories, I guess. A big Rexall drug store on the other corner. A shoe store,

Florsheim, right across the street from me. A red front store, looks like novelties and stuff. . . ." It won't take long. Your friend will know where you are by basic description.

Polysyllabic words are not appropriate in descriptions. You are not trying to confuse the listener, you are trying to identify your idea. Descriptions are sometimes best when childishly simple. The strength may be found in the details themselves: the marks of aging in old bricks, the scars of a beaten tree, the great eyes of a hungry child. Blackboards seldom have elaborate frames. Descriptions are blackboards, just an area on which to enact an illustration. I vote a distinguished honor award to that p/t who has never given up the ghost in the white, wild, embroidered sheets of grandiloquence.

It is also a saving of time and energy to remember that your hearers have both intelligence and imagination. The clear enunciation of a word produces an image in each mind.

Storm
City
Boy
Hill
Train
Horse
Night

Each listener will see for himself what he associates with the word.

If, for some reason, modification is necessary, this can be done and should be done with the minimum.

Rollicking storm
Bright-eyed city
Studious boy

Sculptured hill
Plodding train
Graceful horse
Sullen night

Usually one word can decipher the mood you attach to the picture.

If there is a need to further identify the temper of the predicament, remember that verbs excite a great deal more reaction than multiplied adjectives. Of course, the poet's imagination and effusion are helpful, but not indispensable. The attempt to use images, metaphors, and similes can be very disappointing if you depend only on words. They also require ease in delivery; for if you are awkward or self-conscious in the effort, the effect is negligible or harmful. A good illustration is clear enough in itself without being forced into focus by artificial gimmicks.

The description can be severely limited and yet accomplish the task. But there must be a pattern to the whole enterprise or it will not achieve any purpose. Even patch-quilts have dimensions, straight edges, and a general plan. Get as much reality into this definition as possible. If it involves real people, and if it would not embarrass those people, identify them. Real people in a real town doing real things add authenticity to the setting. If it is indiscreet to actually identify such persons, loan them temporary names, "to protect the innocent"; but try to avoid the *he, she,* and *these people* routine.

Billy Sunday gave me several severe private lectures on the importance of identifying historical events and people. He insisted on accuracy and details. I have not always lived up to his expectations and demands in that area, but I have remembered the lectures: 1929, 1930, 1931, 1933, 1934;

Franklin, Pennsylvania; Wheeling, West Virginia; and Winona Lake, Indiana. Mr. Sunday's hypothesis was that the statement of positive and incontestable fact—such as, Martin Luther was born November 10, 1483, at Eisleben, in the County of Mansfield in Thuringia; he attended school at Magdeburg and attracted the attention of an elderly rich lady of the family of Cotta, who supported him in his literary pursuits—establishes an authority for all the remainder of your illustration. By accurate and detailed information you become acceptable as an authority, and this adds great dignity to the illustration itself.

Writers, preachers, and teachers of a hundred years or more ago labored many an illustration with undetailed or inaccurate data. "I have heard it said," or "History records that," are common openings in the old books. This is not acceptable today. Modern education techniques, radio, television, *Reader's Digest,* and Moody Institute of Science Films have informed the public about every sphere of scientific knowledge. The modern audience includes too many smart little kids, well-read old geezers, and with-it intelligentsia, to parade past them an illustration that may not be only inaccurate but totally false. The progress in electronics, medicine, psychiatry, and every art and science can render your illustration archaic by one news report or the latest issue of *Time.*

Some of the best illustrations are found in the human body, seen through the microscope or telescope, pan-handled from the stockyard or vegetable garden; but the facts must be genuine. The jeopardy is multiplied by isolating your listener not only from your illustration but from the truth you are trying to convey. Some of the best illustrations I know are unusable because I have not been able to substantiate them.

When in a hurry or in a bind for an effective closing punch, panic becomes host to disaster. Memory rakes up a line from another's sermon or a hazy outline of an image projected by a half-forgotten occasion. Usually in such a stricture nothing really takes shape. Facts are jumbled, the narration becomes disjointed, and the application may crumble in your hands. This is why I emphasize the recording of accurate data, the necessity of a system to locate the material, and careful preparation of that material. Sometimes you have to plant it like seed and wait for the harvest. It's worth waiting for.

While documentation is necessary in historical or technical context, it does not have to be heavy or endless. A desire for accuracy may provoke an overdoing of details and a neglect of the point. As too much description can spoil the picture, too much data can choke an application. Blessed is the man who standing in the shoes of the speaker remembers the seat of the listener.

Personal experience is the simplest, most believable, and, therefore, the most effective illustration. The temptation to use such illustrations exclusively is precarious, however. If, ministering to the same group of people, one consistently tells about himself, his wife, his children, his parents, his friends, and his dog, he may provoke a scream of resentment: "Doesn't he ever talk about anything but himself and his family?" We must remember that if p/t's are given to exaggeration, listeners are even more prone to this lack of grace. Two consecutive illustrations from your kitchen will have them reporting to their relatives in rival classes or churches, "I know what they had for dinner at his house every night last year. I also know what detergent they use, how many potholders they have, and what shelf is stacked with catsup and mustard." The extensive use of home-life incidents may also irritate or overly pleasure your family and friends. Your intimates may ostracize you from their normal moods, insisting that you embarrass them; or they may begin preening for their roles and you will find yourself living with Charlie Brown, Blondie, Matt Dillon, or Abby and Ann in one column.

There is no law that insists an illustration must begin by reading its label, complete with contents and weight. I find the opening sentence, "Let me illustrate. . ." holds little inspiration for me or the audience. Television drama is increasingly employing an opening gimmick which may be an actual introduction to the plot or a quick sequence of scenes that will be used in the drama. This snares the attention of the viewer before any announcement of the show, commercials, or other material distracts him. These formats are subject to constant change; but at the moment of this writing, this program formula is in growing use. It can be an exciting adventure to get a running start into an illustration before anyone knows where you are going. There is the stimulation of seeing the hearer follow, wondering where you and he are headed. Finally, he himself walks right into the interpretation. This allows the p/t to be a guide, not just a map, and open an area in which the audience actually participates.

Judgment must be used, of course, in attempting any illustration. The age of the listeners is relevant, for a setting which older people might appreciate could alienate the younger listeners. Children are especially tolerant, however; and if they are given a small amount of attention or material at their level, they apparently forgive you if you spend the balance of the time instructing the mature. Maybe they intuitively know that the adults need the instruction or perhaps they are simply glad to have their parents receiving the stern end of the lecture. In an audience of children only, however, it is a different experience. That built-in four-second wiggle is usually in fine form during a lesson or message. It is humiliating to watch children lie on their tummies in front of a television set and gobble down cartoons without sticking a pin in somebody's bottom or pinching each other in rotation like a mechanical lint-snitcher. It is enough to make an honored man wish that his D.D. meant Donald Duck.

The personal experience which appears like a slice from everybody's experience is the gem worth treasuring. This kind needs nothing but a simple sketch, and everyone is in the picture with you. One of the most effective I have used is generally introduced with a casual question: "Did you ever take a long trip in a car with a couple of youngsters?" That will always make a few heads shake in the affirmative motion and may even make a few nodders jerk to attention. There is always someone who has just returned from such a trip or is planning such a trip. Young people remember one from a few years ago when they were small or one last summer with a smaller brother or sister who was more trouble than an unpaid charge account.

"You were going to visit grandma. A four-day trip across country."

Very few families, and thus very few people, have not indulged in something akin to this kind of trip. As it unfolds, those who have not had such a journey remember seeing a family in a restaurant or a motel who were obviously doing this very thing.

Hooray for the human mind! It is an artist who will fill in many of the blanks for you. Don't leave the picture untended too long, however, or that same mind will put beards and funny glasses on your masterpiece. The action must move swiftly enough to excite and slowly enough that the listener can take what he wants as it goes by.

"You had planned it for weeks, and finally came the day. You decided on a 4:00 A.M. departure in order to get a good start on your first driving day. You were all packed the night before. Father got the car loaded, and the springs burped at the last squeezed-in case. The back seat of the car was evened up with luggage, blankets, and pillows so that the kids could sleep, nice and comfy, for a few hours. Father retired at 10:00. Mother scrubbed the kitchen floor, dusted the house, waxed the family room floor, and retired at 2:00 A.M. She was determined that any burglars during your absence would know she was a good house-keeper. Maybe they'd be ashamed to steal anything."

The narration produces a subtle change of person. Who is telling this story? I or father or mother? Really, you are telling it, whoever you are; and that is exactly what I intended for you to do.

"The alarm scratches against your brain at three-forty-five. You repeat your resolutions to get an early start, hand over heart as though doing the pledge to the flag. You tiptoe around the house as though you're afraid of waking the neighborhood. The sleeping little dolls are carried out to the car and carefully tucked in. They groan, roll over, and snore. You quick-check the house for locked doors, locked windows, turned-off faucets, and a light left burning in the front room. It seems almost sacrilegious to start the motor, and it coughs into the morning air like an old man clearing his throat. Slowly you back into the street, the tail of the car complaining metallically at the gutter. The headlights cut a roving arc across your neighbor's lawn, and then stare down into the black street ahead of you.

"You ease back a little. 'Well, we're on our way. Sure hope those sleepin' beauties stay dead to the world for a couple of hours anyhow.'

"You turn left. Proceed two blocks east. Right turn. At the end of the street you pick up the freeway entrance. Stop sign. And as you are ready to enter the freeway, a head pops up over the back of the front seat, and a small voice asks, 'Are we there yet?' "

Skilled and well-practiced professionals can perfectly imitate a child's voice, but any responsible p/t can achieve a desired effect by control of his nervous system and a modicum of vocal flexibility. In this setting, perfect imitation is not the aim. Children sometimes lisp, garble words, and rush through sentences without emphasis. The question "Are we there yet?" must be clear, deliberate, and preferably spoken slowly. The voice should be pitched as high as possible. Not realism, but the reality of a situation is at stake. Each listener will hear it for himself.

The initial frustration being perpetrated, the p/t is now at liberty to hasten or hold back the action as long as it seems appropriate. "You stop for gas, pull up to a restaurant, check into a motel at night or get a red light in some small town, and each interruption of the journey is embraced with the query, 'Are we there yet?' "

A gesture of irritation, the normal reaction of most adults, will probably produce a few grins, as the answer is snapped, "No, not yet!"

All of this is preparation for the final sequence.

"At last all the miles have ground out under your wheels. The scenery has gone by in a big-as-life production. You're in grandma's town, and you're turning the corner toward grandma's house. You squirm a little, enjoying the luxury of being able to relax, which you haven't done for four days. You smile at each other. 'Good trip. We made good time.'

"You call over your shoulder, 'O.K., kids, here we are, safe and sound. There's grandma's house. The big white one on the corner.'

"It's as quiet as though you asked for volunteers for doing dishes. You look back, and they are curled up, sound asleep, on the seat."

The charm of this simple illustration is its almost universal identification. Every listener is in it with you. It has the blessed advantage of being fun to tell. It almost tells itself. The listener knows what's coming, but he wants it to come. He wants it to happen just as he knows it has to happen. Another joy of this one is the ease of getting into the application. Some captivating ideas are awkward in getting to the point, but this one skips ahead of you.

"How often God's children have asked the Father if we were there yet. Jesus indicated to His questioning disciples that 'It's not for you to know such times and seasons.' But it's hard to be patient. It's a long journey to the house of many mansions.

"Some of the grandest saints and most astute Bible students have approached the question with confidence that they had the answer. It must be now — the Lord must come now for His Church.

"But not yet. Oh, the day will come. God will wheel all His chariots into the driveway. He will bring all of His own safely home. Perhaps some of us will have fallen asleep by then, but He will awaken us with the shout and the trump. We can afford to be patient. We're on the way home."

No apology is necessary for giving an audience cause to smile or laugh. If a blunder produces laughter, this may embarrass a speaker; and there are no patent methods for getting out of such situations. Anyone who speaks frequently will occasionally stumble. Some audiences are forgiving, some are not. There are moments when the noblest course of action is to retreat into a corner, lick your wounds, and wait for the next opportunity. The hazard of facing the same audience is slight, for the previous gathering will be erased like last month's electric bill and they'll be ready to enjoy the illumination without the shadow of your fumble.

Honest laughter, legitimately provoked, is wholesome and encouraging. People who laugh will weep. If the illustration produces laughter, you know you have been heard and understood. Any response is better than no response at all. God help the man who has to speak to a crowd which has mentally gone home.

This is the style of door which I have found to be the most satisfying. It gets to the point quickly and easily. It involves the listener without straining his credibility, and he becomes involved without realizing it. The picture is easy to remember and carry away with you. There are no difficult explanations. It does not require any clever wording or neat turn of a sentence to make it work. The sensational, dramatic epoch has its place; but give me a thousand illustrations with which people can identify, and you may keep the epochs. Bless those kids! They all wake up at the most inconvenient moments and in the most aggravating manner. That's what makes this door move on its hinges.

"An illustration is not a mere prettiness—an ornamental phrase that might be left out without detriment to the train of thought—it is something which really lights up that train of thought itself, and enables the reader or hearer to see the aim, as well as to feel the force, of the logic. An argument may be demonstrative—it may thoroughly establish the position maintained—but it may not at first, and simply as an argument, be fully appreciated; when, the understanding having done its work, passion and genius shall crown the whole with some vivid illustration, which shall make it stand out with a distinctness that shall never be forgotten! It is one great faculty of the mind holding up a lighted torch to the workmanship of another" (Thomas Binney).[5]

[5]R. A. Bertram, *A Homiletic Encyclopaedia of Illustration*, (London: R. D. Dickinson, 1879).

INTERPRETATION

CHAPTER FIVE

INTERPRETATION

This is where it becomes evident I am talking with one hand on a pulpit Bible and not leaning on a bare lectern. This is where the preacher/teacher cannot be abbreviated. It is thinkable that thus far a few ideas might be found in these pages which would be usable for any teacher or for someone appointed to inform the local Kiwanis about sewer gas or even helping to entertain relatives while waiting for the TV repairman to replace a deceased transistor. But, as stated in various terms, this is not a treatise on telling jokes; this is a set of directions for hanging doors and pushing/pulling people through them.

The interpretation of the illustration is ordinarily the final touch. A versatile rhetorician may occasionally be able to install the interpretation before the door is even fitted for the opening, but this may work more confusion than clarity. The interpretation actually has little to do with the door itself. It is primarily concerned with action as contrasted with attention and authority. The interpretation is vitally related to the listener and what he does with the illustration. Inasmuch as this is not a theological or doctrinal discussion to define fine points of scriptural interpretation, the terms used will necessarily be quite general.

Be certain that you do not attempt to suspend your doctrine on the illustration, for no illustration will bear such weight or should be put to such stress. To hazard a dogma on an image can be disastrous. Strange doctrinal positions can be assumed if one premises his doctrine on history, even scriptural history, and stranger yet if one accepts illustrations as teachers of tenets.

It becomes mandatory that anyone using an illustration knows what he believes and what he is trying to convey to others. Because it leads to mental confusion and spiritual inefficiency, it is tragic that many Christians are not doctrinally substantial. It is futile to attempt to affix blame for this. Obviously the Christian who has had the benefit of church ministry, a Bible in his own hands, and the resources available to anyone who is willing to read and study, cannot be held guiltless if he is uncertain and unconvinced of his own doctrinal position. But it compounds the tragedy when a preacher/teacher is unsettled or vague about doctrine, and especially so if he strings his precepts on a series of illustrations rather than skillful use of the Word of God.

These paragraphs are intended to reinforce the original contention that this book is not a substitute for anything. I am not projecting a new system of Bible study, a unique revelation of some obscure passage, or a novel gimmick to be exaggerated into a denominational banner. Before you tackle the illustration of truth, be sure of the truth. This is about doors, not about the foundation.

An illustration is only intended to illustrate. No boast is made that it proves anything. Caution is essential, because you can obliquely illustrate anything. Discernment of the spiritual will depend on the interpretation.

If these sentences seem overly blunt or overly repetitive, I admit to a prejudice about this. There was a time I confounded illustration with proof. I have heard the finest of Bible teachers unwittingly do the same stupid thing. (I beg indulgence for violating my own principle about identifying the actors. Prudence, however, dictates namelessness at this point.)

Great Preacher A.A., a highly rated authority, whose position I accept, insisted that the Church could not go through the Great Tribulation because Lot was taken out of Sodom before the judgment fire fell.

Great Preacher B.B., high esteemed, and especially in his own camp, insisted that there must be two works of grace because Noah sent forth two birds— a raven and a dove— from the ark.

Both A.A. and B.B. put unwarranted strain on their illustrations. A brief look at the contexts immediately disavow what either wanted to state. In the case of A.A., if Lot's escape from Sodom proves the Church will escape the Great Tribulation, we must logically conclude that the Church escapes to a place of incest and the production of a heathen population. This is too ridiculous to deserve rebuttal. In B.B.'s premise about a second work of grace, if the two birds prove this, what about the other birds and beasts? Do they prove umpteen works of grace or umpteen works of sin? Either man could have made the illustration stand up as an illustration, but not as a proof.

Relative to interpretation is a consideration of the necessity of such. A great deal of time and effort is wasted in illustrative material which is denied the right of application. From days when I watched over guppies, angel fish, and snails, I recall a procedure which was intended to preclude shocking the poor fish. There were some detailed instructions about aging water, so that when new water was introduced into the aquarium it was at room temperature. It is possible that some accommodation for room temperature is also necessary in presenting truth to a person or persons. Occasionally one may wish for the shock of startling ideas, but such novelties may not be as effective as one imagines and constant use militates against any degree of efficiency. This subtle practice of meeting room temperature vindicates what is often referred to as "throw-away material." In today's tight time schedules, however, there should be little disposition to make interesting remarks just to fill in time. The human interest story, the quick amusing aside, may sometimes relax both speaker and listeners or may change a mood or provide motion from one area of thought to another. It would be inappropriate to totally condemn all such material; but with the pressure mounting to keep messages to a minimum, there is a necessity to make even the warm-up ideas applicable.

The more experienced and fluent speakers have the greater hazard at this point. There is an almost irresistible urge to keep talking about interesting and enjoyable things that neither illustrate nor illuminate. A reservoir of reading, thinking, writing, and living enrich a man's vocabulary and mind with a wealth of ideas to pin on the lapel of any discussion. The irrelevant remarks can become deadly. If, used properly, they provide an opportunity for listeners to chew and swallow what has been said, used improperly they break the continuity of concentration and allow the minds to go wandering off over the hills instead of staying with the group.

Hypercriticism would be indelicate here, for all of us have unintentionally given our listeners a chance to depart without dismissal. I recently heard a well-known and very capable radio minister discussing Christ as the Bread of Life. He suddenly launched into a description of a visit he had made to a restaurant in New York, which specialized in serving all kinds of bread. It was interesting: I could smell the freshly baked loaves, steaming with goodness. I saw the thin bread sticks, savored the tangy cheese flavor in some, delightful onion in others. But I wondered what was the point? To my amazement, there was no application made of this. He had a parable without interpretation. It was an unrelated segment of an excellent Bible exposition. Having found myself guilty of this same aimlessness, I considered the possibilities: (1) he forgot the interpretation or carelessly ran on and forgot to give it; (2) he slipped in the sketch as a last-minute idea without plan. If (1), he was guilty of inadequate preparation. If (2), he wasted time, effort, and what could have been a good illustration if properly applied.

Inasmuch as this one was left in midair, I presume it was unplanned. Unplanned illustrations, like unwashed children, should be left at home until there is opportunity to make them more presentable and usable.

The bridge from the illustration itself to the interpretation must not be shaky or ill defined. I find it profitable to read frequently Nathan's perfect pinpointing of the target, David, according to II Samuel 12. The illustration was perfect, and the interpretation was worthy of it. Nathan was sent of God to David, but I must remember that I have been sent of God to men. I may not be as well informed of personal sins, but I am aware that I speak to sinners. If they were perfect people God would not dispatch me to speak to them. News reports tell me quite plainly the condition of society in general, and any communication with human hearts reveals unrest, guilt, and disillusionment. There is a need to consider a man's relationship to God.

Nathan had the perfect attention getter. He confronted a political leader with the inequalities in his society. The rich and the poor paraded through that throne room. Sympathy was aroused. An outrageous act was described. A miserable injustice clapped like thunder for the notice of the king. Nathan got a response. It is possible this is a greater miracle than Pentecost; for when you preach to just one and receive 100 percent response, that is a miracle beyond all other miracles.

Nathan's masterful handling of the interpretation makes the record invaluable. I see the point of the story as I read it. I think David saw the point. But David probably thought Nathan wouldn't dare to bring the sword from the scabbard and drive it into the ruler's heart. Perhaps he thought Nathan would say, "Think about it!" as they do with those clever contemporary antismoking spots.

The lightninglike maneuver of Nathan's rhetoric indicates there was a higher hand on Nathan's mind and spirit. "Thou art the man!" echoed and bounced back from every wall into the heart of David. The tale of the rich and poor, the tears over the dear little lamb, the threat to see justice done—all these were God's way of getting the aim. I must bear in my soul the truth that I speak to men whom God is after: He wants something, and I am His hand or voice or finger to get His Word to them. David didn't ask Nathan who was the villain that perpetrated the awful deed. I reread the record and wonder if Nathan had been prepared for David's quick and violent reaction. Maybe David suspected what the application would be and was trying to preclude the lightning from striking him. While David talked of righting the wrong, Nathan waded in, splashing the conviction. He had the interpretation worded ahead of time.

This is not a game of tiddlywinks. We are not given the opportunity to keep flipping the bright discs all around the living room rug until they land in the cup out of sheer weariness. Although there is much disdain of preaching as either an art or a ministry, the Scriptures conclude that "it pleases God by the foolishness of preaching to save them that believe." Define preaching as anything and everything from a dialogue to a lecture, from a testimony to a flannelgraph, from a radio skit to a street corner amplifier, the fact remains that there is a necessity, a God-ordained device, of facing men with the truth as it is in Jesus and presenting the claims of the Lord Christ as crucified and risen. In this dramatic encounter of men with the Word of God, there is a moment of destiny. Every critical task has at least one point at which error is tragic and irremediable. A physician, a mechanic, a pilot, a gardener, a driver—each face moments when there is no margin for error. A p/t may kick language around by its parenthetical interpolations and commit grammarcide with disregard for sensitive listeners; he may read the text falteringly, blunder on proper names, and pinch back his outline every time it comes to flower as though trying to get it to grow a broader base; but the real failure is to miss the interpretation. And probably that is the only real failure. This is not an area where you can permit the hearer to think for himself.

There is a subtle insinuation in Romans 6:17, "Ye have obeyed from the heart that form of doctrine which was delivered you." Weymouth enlightens it: "You have now yielded a hearty obedience to that system of truth in which you have been instructed." The flat statement not to allow the hearer to think for himself sounds radical, but that is the very purpose for the assembling of persons and for their choice of listening to you or whoever is teaching. In this concept God and man have combined to ordain a man for the proclamation of the Word of God. "The Lord has said" is the authority by which we announce truth or, as Paul defines it, "that system of truth." The trumpet with the faltering, ill-defined tone is rejected by New Testament logic: "In case the trumpet emits an indistinct call, who will get ready for battle?" (I Cor. 14:8 Berkeley). Therefore, conviction to the ultimate of certainty must be experienced by the p/t without the illustration to bolster his argument; and the illustration simply helps him to hang a door for the listener to see how to get into the truth revealed.

The above quotation from Romans 6 alludes to the ritual of baptism as a clearly enunciated Christian ceremony. The spiritual meanings which were figured "in likeness" illustrate the system of truth which the apostles insist they have received with adequate instruction. Therefore, they have yielded obedience to that system. This is not an apology for poorly tutored believers who follow any and every leader, but this is a plea for better indoctrination so that Christians will know exactly where they stand and why they assume that position. Such a stance begins with a convinced and convincing teacher.

The emphasis on educated personnel and the increase of the well-informed, well-read population who are not afraid to ask questions, make it more important today than at any point of church history for a teacher to be doctrinally secure. Evidently many preachers of a hundred years ago were not pressed with some areas of doctrine which are open debate today. Perhaps they were under other pressures, but until the widespread recognition of liberalism as such, the carefully worded texts of doctrinal precision were not important to the average listener. It is possible that there was more simple, genuine, whole-hearted faith in the Word of God and a less elaborate analysis of the preacher or teacher. Spurgeon was a precisionist in the art of doctrine, and his position is crystal clear; but some of the publicized preachers of the past eras were masters of preaching rather than of doctrine. Beecher, Talmage, Brooks, Guthrie, and others were magnificent; but their doctrinal posture was not carefully defined. Therefore, many of the old books of illustrations contain items which generally convey a truth, but which specifically say something so contrary to doctrinal purity that they are unusable.

Several old preachers use an incident, the actual origin of which is impossible to pinpoint. Usually it is told in the first person. The minister encountered a boy who had a bird in a cage. The bird was terrified. The boy was adamant on one point: he would not release the bird. (Obviously this occurred in a day when birds, dogs, cats, mice, hamsters, and fighting tropical fish could not be purchased in shopping malls and paid for through a bank credit card at 1½ percent per month.)

The narrator bargained with the boy to buy the bird. When the bird was paid for, the liberator released the bird and watched it fly away, free and happy. It is presumed that the boy was given back the empty cage and sallied forth to catch another bird and sell to another bird lover.

This is a delightful story, and it makes all the listeners feel virtuous. They have sympathized with the bird and the bird's rescuer. I have heard it told with the mean expressions of the boy showing on the curled lip and in the gleaming eye of the teller. I have heard the frightened chirpings of the bird and the clink of silver into the boy's palm. The cage door has clicked open before my very eyes, and the bird took off, beating his wings awkwardly, until he could regain his song and his flight. The story ends just as you want it to end.

Then comes the interpretation.

Then comes confusion.

"I was in bondage, as terrified as that bird. Satan had me caged by sin and self. I knew I couldn't save myself from the devil. But Jesus came, and He saw my plight, paid for my release, and set me free."

Suspicion of this application will be interpreted as sanctified nit-picking—perhaps without sanctification. But today's logical analysts will take it apart. In general terms the application is true. Jesus sets us free from sin and death. He breaks the power of Satan in the life of the individual: in fact, "For this purpose the Son of God was manifested, that he might destroy the works of the devil" (I John 3:8). But the details can be embarrassing: did Jesus pay off Satan? Is this salvation or blackmail? Does Jesus pay our redemption one by one?

This may appear to be an unnecessary extension of a heartwarming story, but realistically this day of intellectualism, doubt, and doctrinal uncertainty demands a careful scrutiny of material. I have been surprised to find young people critical of gospel ministry and scriptural interpretation presented in films, books, music, and tracts, as well as sermons, for using devices which they readily accept as legitimate in fiction, television, theater, and even news reporting. Despite the moral and spiritual laxness of this culture, there is a high demand for consistency and legitimacy in gospel presentation.

This demand is not entirely mischievous. While it may not be possible to avoid all such disparities and weaknesses, and it may eliminate some fascinating items we enjoy. It will also make us more discerning and more exacting with ourselves and our doctrine.

Another angle in interpretation is the selection of which tack to take. Ordinarily this is settled arbitrarily, because the given illustration is only good from one approach. But few speakers—especially when in their most fruitful and useful period—can afford to stockpile good ideas and wait for occasions to use them. Fortunately, good illustrations can be bent—it is a secret hope you can bend it to where you need it. Experience and observation of others are the strong assets in this department. It is tragic to waste a good illustration by a weak application, but this is not necessary and should be avoided. If it is perilous to make an illustration carry a weight it is not capable of supporting, it is equally foolish, even if not so hazardous, to use an illustration with no weight at all.

While having lunch with my mother she reminisced about her Aunt Esther. I had heard about Aunt Esther since I was a child. She was the glamor girl of the family through Grandpa Moline's side of the house. She was also the eccentric or, in modern jargon, the kook.

My mother had often recited the virtues and follies of Aunt Esther. What a character for an illustration! She is everybody's relative. Like her brother, my mother's father, she was an artist—and she was weird. Today she would have had three psychiatrists. She would not put her foot on a third step going up or down stairs. She counted, "One, two," and hopped to the fourth. She refused to use the word *red,* and, seeing me as a baby, she described my hair as lurid. What a ghost in everybody's castle!

Aunt Esther, my mother informed me, wore beautiful clothes which she designed and made herself. She traveled in rather high society in Chicago, graced some events in the Potter Palmer mansion, and shocked the traditionalists with extreme fashions. One feature was never altered, however. She always wore long sleeves which extended over her fingers, resembling half-gloves, with the ends of the sleeves exotically scalloped and jeweled. Her appearance at the top of an old-fashioned staircase, sweeping downward gracefully with a great banister, gave the socially-in a gasp of surprise and admiration. They gossiped her exploits in the carriages on the way home and poisoned her style while sipping tea in the drawing room the next day. Then they called their dressmakers and demanded something more daring than Esther Moline would wear. Aunt Esther couldn't have cared less if the Katzenjammer Kids had been adopted by Happy Hooligan and moved in with Maggie and Jiggs. She was inured to society's reaction. They thought her talented, brilliant, and nutty; but she was guarding her own secret.

Those long sleeves with the elaborately decorated half-glove effect were her invention by necessity. Aunt Esther suffered from what was then called rheumatism. She had greatly swollen, red knuckles. She was too proud to display her misshapen hands and too artistic to suffer the indignities of a bandage. Therefore, she covered the unsightly knuckles with careful stitching, brilliant beads, and intricate design.

Everybody has a relative of which he is half-proud and half-ashamed. I knew this identification was attention getting. Aunt Esther would project colorslides of Aunt Turfnose or Second Cousin Hodpuss. No family should be without one. Conversation about them fills great gaps of empty time at family reunions, weddings to which you're invited to use up the invitations, and graduation exercises you attend because somebody sent your youngster a pencil box when he graduated into ninth grade.

The real decision about such a human interest item is what to do about the application. There are two—opposite to each other, and both perfectly clear. There is the ready-made interpretation that people try to cover up the truth about themselves. Aunt Esther's exaggerated sleeves and their fancy fashion fooled her more than they fooled others. Her family, friends, doctor, and probably a lot of others knew about the swollen knuckles and the mechanism used to hide them from sight.

That kind of application, however, is fairly easy to find. Usually news reports, the wig shop, the cosmetic counter, and your own wardrobe can provide an illustration of this order on demand. There was a more subtle and, I thought, stronger application in provoking sympathy for Aunt Esther. We all have sympathy for the odd characters in other people's family trees. It is our own kith-and-kin cranks that are hard to bear. Probably because of guilt for past rudeness or impatience, everyone feels sympathy for his own relatives when they are somewhere else. It is easy to love your in-laws when they stay a thousand miles away.

The Word admonishes that we should care for and shield each other. We are all baptized by one Spirit into the body of Christ. Swollen knuckles are not uncommon. Cover them! If we deal harshly with our fellow Christians we may miss the opportunity God has given us to cover a multitude of sins rather than to expose them for the amusement of the unbelieving world.

Neither interpretation does violence to Scripture. Both are reminders of human imperfections. One is kinder than the other, and perhaps in that context serves a nobler purpose. It is not good policy, however, to attempt to get both applications at the same time nor to return later to the same group using the illustration again with the other emphasis.

An old dear from my youth unrolled a fragrant and colorful memo with me of the candy store where we squandered a penny on the delights of childhood. The candy store lady would usually patiently wait while you rubbed your finger down the whole length of the glass case, vocalizing the merits of each of the confections. If the little shop happened to entertain an adult who would buy a whole dime's worth of licorice or maybe one of those gaudy boxes, beneath whose painted lid there reposed a mixture of bonbons and jordan almonds, the merchantess of the mints might be inclined to hurry you up so she could make the larger sale. But there was a mingled rapture and agony in the irrevocable decision. If you wanted quantity you went for jujubes or cinnamon red hots or candy corn or, around Valentine's Day, the hearts on which were printed remarkable legends, such as, "Oh, you kid!" "Watch my smoke!" or "O.K." For quality you looked longingly at a wax bottle filled with sweet syrup or the large size green leaves or the jawbreaker that you sucked down to several colors before you reached the tiny center that dissolved with a puff of sweetness.

Once the penny had been exchanged for the goods, however, there was no changing the choice. You had to stick with what you had selected, even if it wasn't as flavorful as you had anticipated.

Choice of interpretation of an illustration brings the same frustration. The decision has to be made how to use the idea; and once it is used, the energy has been spent, as far as that group of listeners is concerned. Some of us who are fortunate enough to move from crowd to crowd do get a reprieve on this and can use the item again, hoping to improve the application. It is often proved, however, that the tootsie roll is not a better choice than the three yellow bananas that taste like paint.

Illustrative material may appear to be trite, frivolous, superficial, and mere padding; but experience has demonstrated to many of us that the best remembered of all spoken material is the illustration. I have watched my best arguments, philosophical conclusions, and spiritual polemics leave no visible trace on human consciousness; but I have found my message still living in the picture of a small boy with a broken bag, the image of an old field laden with weeds, and the classic outlines of an ancient car that wheezed through traffic with a noble disregard for speed and power.

In the *Memoir of Rowland Hill* there is the record of two men who entered Surrey Chapel to hear the well-publicized eccentric preacher. One of the two was preparing to leave shortly for India. He was a man "without God and without hope." His friend was a consistent Christian, earnestly desiring to lead the unbeliever to Christ. The Christian had resolutely worked on the other to get him to attend church the last four Sunday nights before departing for India.

The non-Christian had attended church three Sunday nights in a row. Many were praying for him. But the fourth Sunday night was on the scene, and the untouched was still untouched. That fourth and final Sunday the Christian was a bundle of anxiety. He had prayed. He had wept. His friend wanted to hear Rowland Hill, and thus they turned to Surrey Chapel. The Christian was secretly praying, however, that Mr. Hill would be on good behavior, in a solemn state of mind, and that God would prohibit the preacher from indulging in what some termed his extreme and ridiculous remarks.

Hill was eighty-six at the time. You would think such a venerable old man would give proper attention to the proprieties of the ministry. But the extraordinary pulpiteer announced his text, a tirade against the devil, "We are not ignorant of his devices." Wasting no time, Hill launched into a description of a scene in the street: a drove of pigs, which were not driven, but which quietly followed their leader. "This singular fact excited my curiosity, and I pursued the swine, until they all quietly entered the butchery. I then asked the man how he succeeded in getting the poor, stupid, stubborn pigs to follow him so willingly. He told me the secret. He had a basket of beans under his arm, and kept dropping them as he proceeded. Ah! my dear hearers, the devil has his basket of beans, and he knows how to suit his temptation to every sinner. He drops them by the way, and the poor sinner is thus led captive by the devil at his own will, and if the grace of God prevent not, he will get him at last into his butchery, and there he will keep him forever. Oh, it is because 'we are not ignorant of his devices' that we are anxious this evening to guard you against them."

The Christian mourned deeply about the tale of the

pigs. He calculated that it was shallow, perhaps vulnerable to all kinds of intellectual and even scriptural criticism, and that maybe it would produce a laugh instead of a sober concept of God and eternity and salvation. Yet as the two men left the chapel, the unbeliever remarked, "What a singular statement we had tonight about the pigs, and yet how striking and convincing it was." His subsequent letters revealed that the pigs and the basket of beans had made an impression and produced the result the Christian had prayed for, but which he really hoped would come from a more conventional picture.

An extra benefit of using the common to illustrate the spiritual is that it turns each discerning person into a commentator or expositor of the truth. There are dangers in such liberty; but the advantages far outweigh the hazard, if the illustrative concept is caught from a discriminating p/t. This may appear to contradict the earlier statement that you dare not allow the listener to think for himself; yet it is only an extension of that same premise. Under your teaching, as a disciple or learner, the hearer cannot be allowed to think for himself until he has learned to think for himself by learning Christ (Eph. 4:20); and that is why he is under your teaching. If your work is well done, he will emerge to see the truth buttoned into every garment, singing at every corner, and hollowed into the rut of every wheel.

There is a loud demand, and rightly so, for Christianity to be lived in the everyday setting. Faith cannot be a cloistered tenant in a sanctuary far from duty and desire, and yet exist as a potent force in the lives of men.

Dr. F. D. Huntington echoes down the long tunnel of a century: "We want a Christianity that is Christian across counters, over dinner tables, behind the neighbor's back as in his face. We want a Christianity that we can find in the temperance of the meal, in moderation of dress, in respect for authority, in amiability at home, in veracity and simplicity in mixed society. We want fewer gossiping, slandering, gluttonous, peevish, conceited, bigoted Christians. To make them effectual, all our public religious measures, institutions, benevolent agencies, missions, need to be managed on a high-toned, scrupulous, and unquestionable scale of honor, without evasion or partisanship, or overmuch of the serpent's cunning. The hand that gives away the Bible must be unspotted from the world. The money that sends the missionary to the heathen must be honestly earned. In short, both the arms of the Church—justice and mercy—must be stretched out, working for man, strengthening his brethren, or else your faith is vain, and ye are yet in your sins."

Many of the details, much of the language, and some of the terms and emphasis of this paragraph would be altered in today's intellectual, permissive, and sophisticated society, but the basic plea would remain: we want a Christianity that can be lived every day. It must be possible to integrate the fact of faith and the person of Christ into life or this gospel will have no relevance for this generation's impatient people. There is no better way to institute the truth into experience and conduct than to imprint every common street with a translation of the Bible and make each area of life, from infancy to death, a seminary library in which we read and hear the voice of God. As those of us who minister in His name employ these at-hand applications, those who learn will be tutored by the Holy Spirit to discern such parables administered in each dimension of life. It's easier to hang doors when there's more than one on the job.

KREGEL PULPIT AIDS

PASTORAL TEACHING OF PAUL
William Edward Chadwick

Of what does a pastoral ministry consist? We're seeing principles replaced by methods and success being measured by statistics. What is the right way, the biblical answer? Warren W. Wiersbe, in the Foreword, wrote, "Because of this confusion, I rejoice that this work *Pastoral Teaching of Paul* is now available to a generation of ministers who need what these chapters present. After all, Paul was not only a great preacher, missionary and theologian, he was a great *pastor!* It is time our present ministerial generation recovered the pastoral vision of the Apostle Paul." This book is based on the pastoral *ministry* of Paul as recorded in the Book of Acts and revealed in his epistles.

65 WAYS TO GIVE EVANGELISTIC INVITATIONS
Faris D. Whitesell

In this unique book, many types of invitations are examined and classified to be readily referred to and used. Every issue and fear is dealt with in regard to giving invitations, and valued instruction is given to enable you to become an effective fisherman. What a valued treasure you will find in this exhaustive work on the "invitation."

HOW TO FIND AND DEVELOP EFFECTIVE ILLUSTRATIONS
Louis Paul Lehman

In this practical handbook on the use of illustrations, the speaker, teacher, and preacher are challenged to develop this skill of seeing, thinking and plucking illustrative material from everyday sights, sounds and objects. Here is a wealth of useful help in this unique book.